Waskesiu and its Neighbours

A Casual Illustrated History

Graham A. MacDonald / Grit McCreath

***Waskesiu** and its Neighbours*
A Casual Illustrated History

Library and Archives Canada Cataloguing in Publication

MacDonald, Graham A. (Graham Alexander), 1944-
Waskesiu and its neighbours : a casual illustrated history / Graham A. MacDonald, Grit McCreath.

Includes bibliographical references and index.
ISBN 978-1-55383-183-9

1. Waskesiu Lake Region (Sask.)--History. 2. Prince Albert National Park (Sask.)--History. 3. Outdoor recreation--Saskatchewan--Waskesiu Lake Region--History. 4. Outdoor recreation--Saskatchewan--Prince Albert National Park--History. I. McCreath, Grit (Margrit S.), 1948- II. Title.

FC3514.P75M33 2008 971.24'2 C2008-900873-1

Book Design by Lori Nunn
nunn@agt.net
Canmore, AB

Printed in Canada by Friesens Corporation
Altona, Manitoba

Dedication

To everyone who has visited Prince Albert National Park country
and who remembers the experience with warm affection

Table of Contents

Canoe crews ‘poling’ by using four metre (twelve foot) spruce poles, in the proposed Prince Albert National Park area, probably on the Montreal or Waskesiu River. c. 1926.

The original image here was retouched in colour for a glass lantern slide from a black and white photograph. The negative was first printed on glass and then hand-tinted with transparent colours.

Lac
La Ronge
Prince Albert
National Park
Prince Albert
North Battleford
Saskatoon

Of the great system of public reservations set aside in our National Parks, we as Canadians may be justly proud. They are preserving for future generations typical examples of our original Canada and providing for the people of today vast playgrounds of unspoiled nature where wild animals and plant life is protected and where people are free to camp and fish and enjoy those healing and vitalizing influences of Nature which in our increasingly strenuous and industrialized life become more and more necessary to well-being.

This latest addition to this system is the Prince Albert National Park, which sets aside a typical example of that rich lake and woodland region lying in the northern part of the Province of Saskatchewan. Rich in historic interest and the romance of the early days of pioneer exploration and the fur trade, the new park possesses, in its chain of beautiful lakes and streams, opportunities for giving health and enjoyment to thousands while as the gateway to that vast maze of waterways stretching away to two oceans, it seems destined to become a region presenting an irrestistible lure to the canoeist and lover of the wilds.

- W. L. Mackenzie King.
Foreword to the first Park Guide (1928)

WASKESIU
From Songs of Lake Waskesiu
by
Alfred Nicholson
H. PIHL
PUBLISHED & DISTRIBUTED
BY
ALFRED NICHOLSON
NICHOLSON APARTMENTS
SASKATOON
Copyright 1932

Introduction

The Reality of this Place: Introducing Prince Albert National Park

Prince Albert National Park, in its 80th year, still remains rather unknown to most Canadians. Depending on your point of view, its advantage or disadvantage is that it lies somewhat off the beaten track. Bill Waiser, in his fine history of the Park, argues that its identity is locally understood as 'Saskatchewan's Playground.' The name of the Park's main settlement, Waskesiu, is derived from the Cree language for red deer, the term fur traders first used to describe the elk. Since the birth of the Park, Waskesiu has been a favoured summer resort, particularly for those dwelling in the north and central parts of the province. Just as certainly, it has exerted a strong pull on many from away, people who have taken time to discover its secrets and who make the return trip from distant quarters. The reasons for this loyalty and affection have been entertainingly explored in the works of Dorell Taylor. As a long-time Waskesiu observer, she has documented the case that the Park does not have just one, but many realties. Our present trip must be a brief one, and by emphasizing the lesser known visual record of those who have actively 'made history' or been its witnesses, it is the hope of the authors that certain 'less travelled' trails and waterways may be opened for your enjoyment, inspection and inspiration.

As with all parts of Canada, the history here is both ancient and new. Since 1928 the townsite of Waskesiu has dominated the story of the Park. For reasons official and economic, it has remained appropriately small in scale as a settlement and has acted as a seasonal window upon a land which, come fall, tends to then slip out of view once again until the following summer. It is as if the town has been returned for safekeeping to the Park staff who now live there year-round. Augustus Kenderdine and the artists who followed him to take up seasonal residence at nearby Emma Lake always understood that there remains so much more to see . . . next year.

1

Before the Park

The mix of forests and waters in Prince Albert National Park disguise an ancient geological past. Today, the Park area is defined by a subtle height of land including lakes and streams separating two major river valleys, the Churchill to the north and the Saskatchewan to the south. Remnants and actions of the most recent ice age endure at many places in the park. Fine sand beaches, long 'moraine' ridges deposited by melting ice, large 'erratic' boulders sitting where they seemingly should not be, and many other features, give evidence of the glaciers' work. These remains are souvenirs of the last in a series of advances and retreats by great ice sheets across most of what is Canada today.

This glacial era ended about ten thousand years ago. What geologists label the 'Pleistocene Period' started about three million years ago and it was one of what might be called 'global colding' when glacial epochs came and went with regularity. Geologist A. H. Lang noticed that prior to the most recent of these ice-induced geological disruptions, still evident on the surface features of Prince Albert National Park, the essential pattern of the land forms below was essentially the same. During several millions of years prior to the onset of the Pleistocene Period, erosion had reduced the regional land surface to a condition 'more or less like the one seen today.' At the very end of those much warmer 'Tertiary' times, the valley of the Saskatchewan ran roughly in its present course. To be sure, however, the following great ages of glaciers did shuffle the land surface a good deal and Prince Albert National Park golfers will find themselves playing over low ridges of moraine material laid down by the retreating ice.

What a contrast geological and human history provides! People are very recent arrivals in this shifting landscape picture. The human use of the land in these parts has always been rather low-key. Nevertheless, there is a long history pre-dating the European period of settlement. The fragments of evidence for occupations and use over the last six or seven thousand years are few enough, but much has been learned in recent years. The most consistent image is that the lands of Prince Albert National Park served earlier peoples as a kind of 'commons.' For centuries it was a place of resort for various groups from both the south and the north, engaged in following the dictates of a recurring 'seasonal round' in search of fish, game and edible plants. Just who came when was a function of long term climate patterns. There is much interest in 'global warming' in our own day, but such periods have occurred on the Northern Plains before, especially between roughly 8,500 and 4,500 years before the present. This lengthy so-called 'Altithermal' period was marked by warmer and dryer temperatures throughout the Great Plains in both the United States and Canada. For much of this time, the treeline, which today runs well south of the Park, had advanced northward to about the level of Montreal Lake. Thus, much drier grassland prairies extended well into the southern half of the Park.

The archaeologist's spade has turned over stone implements associated with very early groups of bison hunters in the central reaches of the Park. Also found are traces of peoples who were oriented to the valley of the Saskatchewan River and a way of life associated more with fishing and local plant gathering possibilities. Finally, we know something about early peoples from the Churchill River Valley who were more accustomed to pursue the woodland caribou. In cooler periods the caribou trekked further south in the fall than they do today, but probably abandoned the area of Prince Albert National Park in warmer times when the more heavily forested areas to the north would provide a better seasonal habitat.

These patterns of land use waxed and waned over the centuries, giving firm identities to First Nation groups. Distinctive traits and preferences among Native peoples were noticed by European fur traders when they started to enter the region more frequently in the later 18th century. As they penetrated ever further up the Saskatchewan River, the traders encountered diverse peoples, such as the Cree, Assiniboine and Blackfoot, well adapted to the mixed woodlands and prairies. Similarly, traders moving up the Churchill, or English River as it was often called, encountered the more northerly Chipewyan, long adjusted to the pursuit of caribou in the boreal forests and on the open tundra.

Subdivisions of geologic time			Apparent ages (millions of years before the present)
Eras	Periods	Epochs	
Cenozoic	**Quaternary**	**Holocene Pleistocene**	3.0
	Tertiary	Pliocene	13
		Miocene	25
		Oligocene	35
		Eocene	58
		Paleocene	65
Mesozoic	Cretaceous		135
	Jurassic		180
	Triassic		225
Paleozoic	Permian		280
	Pennsylvanian		310
	Mississippian		340
	Devonian		400
	Silurian		430
	Ordovician		500
	Cambrian		600
Precambrian			4.5 billion

The Geological Time Scale showing how recent in earth time is the Pleistocene Period and the ages of ice.

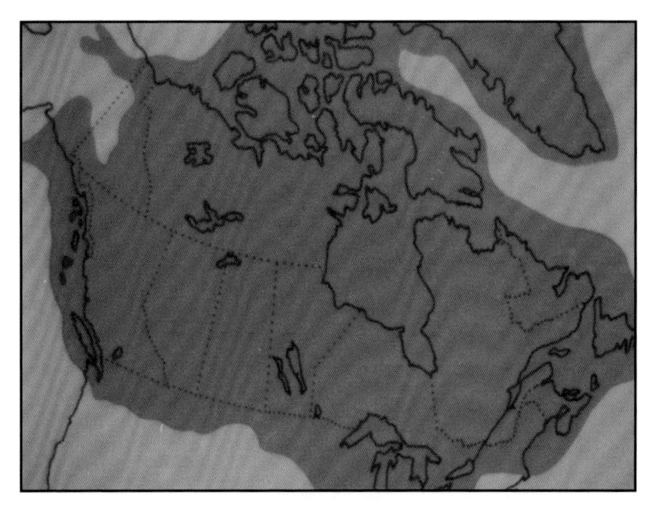

The approximate maximum southern extension of the last major North American glaciation. By ten thousand years ago the ice had retreated back into the high Arctic.

Waskesiu Golf Course. Waskesiu. The ridge is part of a geological moraine of rocky debris deposited during the retreat of the last glaciers. The famous 'lobstick' tree after which several annual golf tournaments are named is visible as the trademark of the first hole.

View of the First Narrows of Waskesiu Lake, 1981. The forest cover and higher shoreline may be compared to that on the opposite page, an imaginative reconstruction of how the landscape may have appeared over a thousand years ago, under warmer conditions.

This finely crafted projectile point, found in the Park, is representative of Besant Culture peoples. Archaeological evidence suggests these peoples hunted plains bison but were also adjusting to woodland occupations of fishing and small game hunting. This point is about 3x1.5 in (7x4 cm).

'Ancient Waskesiuians': Hunting and Fisher Folk of the Narrows. This artistic reconstruction of the Narrows setting, by Jim Webb, shows the site as it might have been experienced by members of the Besant Culture which flourished from about 2000 to 1200 years before the present in the Prairie/Parkland belt. The country is more open as a result of the intentional setting of fire which helped stimulate better bison and game habitat. The Narrows would also have been an ideal place for fishing then, as today, with good water access to the boreal woodlands to the north.

In the years after 1774 competition became very intense between the Hudson's Bay Company and an ever-shifting constellation of fur trading 'pedlars from Quebec' – the most famous group of which formed themselves into the North West Company in 1779. The central business idea of these Montreal-based traders was that useful and not so useful goods should be taken directly to the source, the trappers within the various inland tribes. This would save the Native hunters the trouble of having to make the long annual journey downstream to the competing houses of the Hudson's Bay Company at Cumberland House or to the other posts on Hudson Bay. The lands around today's Park were located directly between the two river valleys which were the main theatres of commercial struggle. It was by these same valleys that ambitious traders, such as the New Englander, Peter Pond, strove to move further and further inland towards 'the captivating Athabasca' with its rich, untapped fur lands. This obscure but fascinating and map-obsessed trader had connections with the lands around Prince Albert National Park, connections which still survive in archaeological form.

The Sturgeon River rises in the central portion of the Park and flows south to meet the North Saskatchewan just a few kilometres west of the City of Prince Albert. It was here that Pond, a much travelled and seasoned trader from Connecticut, now in league with Montreal merchants, arrived in 1776 and established Sturgeon Fort. The buildings have long since disappeared but the locale was commemorated in 1951 by a National Historic Site plaque located near Shellbrook. After 1960 archaeology was conducted in the environs of the old post although much of the original terrain has disappeared into the Saskatchewan River, the result of erosion of the river banks.

Pond wintered for two years at Sturgeon Fort before making his famous advances into the Athabasca country far to the northwest. In 1781 and 1782 he was again closer at hand, wintering at Lac la Ronge, apparently unable to get back to the Athabasca in those seasons, the rivers bound early by freeze-up. Then associated with the firm of McBeath, Ellice & Co., his reputation came under a cloud in connection with the murder of his associate, Étienne Waden, a deed for which many held Pond accountable despite his acquittal in a Montreal court. Pond's remaining fur trade years were spent in the Athabasca and Great Slave Lake regions where his cartographic achievements were significant. If his maps were erroneous on some important points, they still proved to be of singular importance in preparing Sir Alexander Mackenzie for his more famous explorations to the Arctic and Pacific Oceans. Remarkably, Pond was implicated in a second murder in 1787, one for which he was probably not accountable. The scandal was enough, however, to force him from the ranks of the North West Company. He retired back to New England in 1790 where he later wrote his memoirs.

Archaeological investigation at Pond's Sturgeon Fort. (1961). Extensive archaeological work has been conducted at the site of Pond's old fort at the confluence of the Sturgeon and North Saskatchewan Rivers. The efforts have been of a documentary and 'salvage' nature as the river has steadily eroded away most of the original site. The National Historic Sites Plaque erected in 1951 was relocated in 2003 to a location on the old railway right-of-way near Shellbrook.

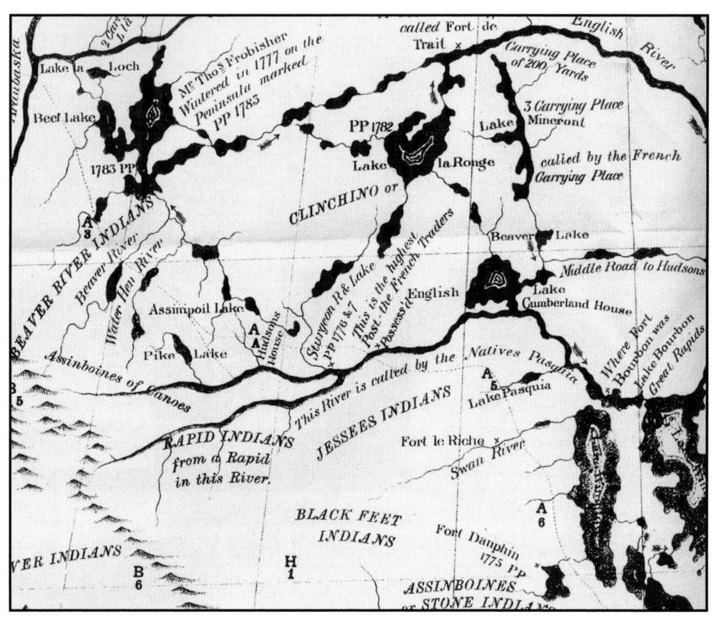

Peter Pond's Map. 1785. This portion of a larger map shows interesting detail on the future area of Prince Albert National Park. The site of Pond's trading post is identified as PP 1776 &7 at the mouth of the Sturgeon River. He has also annotated his post at La Ronge as PP 1782.

Many other fur traders of note frequented the vicinity of the Park, including the explorer and map-maker David Thompson. While with the Hudson's Bay Company, he helped establish South Branch House in 1786 before serving at Manchester House further up the Saskatchewan River. Having joined the North West Company in 1797, he frequented the country around Île à la Crosse in 1798 where he first met Charlotte Small, daughter of 'Nor'wester' Partner Patrick Small and his wife, a Cree woman whose name remains unknown. In the same year he was at Green Lake, some distance to the west of the Park, about halfway between the two great river valleys. This was a jumping off point for the Beaver River and the Lac La Biche country. In 1799 he returned to Île à la Crosse where he married young Charlotte, commencing a long life of mutual adventure and domestic happiness.

Various fur posts on the North Saskatchewan remained important over the next half century, mainly as provisioning posts for the trade which was moving steadily northwest into the fur-rich Athabasca country. By 1821, the intense rivalry of the two main fur companies came to an end with their amalgamation. Fewer posts were hence required. Local trapping went on in the country north of Prince Albert for some time, but by 1830 the post at Lac la Ronge had closed its doors owing to a depletion of fur-bearing animals. The ribbon of land between the two great river valleys remained obscure to Euro-Canadian eyes for many years to come.

Beaver Club Medal of Peter Pond. Membership in the Montreal club was reserved for those fur traders who had 'wintered' in 'le pays en haut' — the far northwest country. On the lower edge is a date signifying the year of the member's first wintering over, in this case, 1769.

Cree peoples. Cumberland House area. This excellent picture was made in 1819 by Lieutenant Robert Hood, a member of the First British Arctic Land Expedition led by Sir John Franklin.

Stanley Mission. Lac la Ronge. The old Village of Stanley Mission was founded in 1852 by the Rev. Robert Hunt, working for the Church Missionary Society. He selected a site on the north shore of the English (Churchill) River for a mission to the Cree, a location only accessible by water. A Hudson's Bay Company carpenter and two Cree men built him a home and school and dwellings for their own families. Construction began on Holy Trinity Church in 1854 and it was completed in 1860.

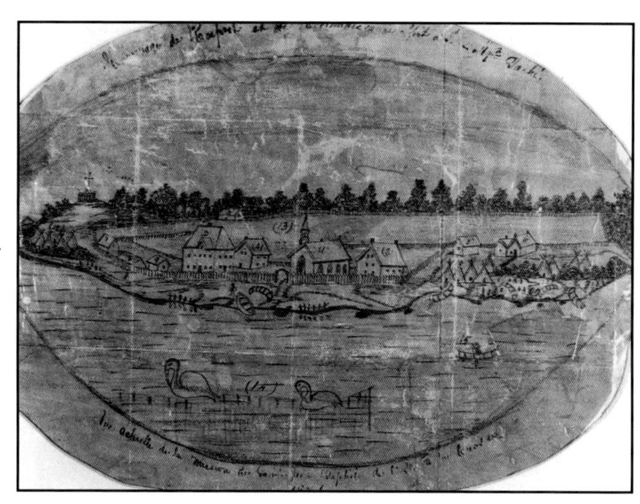

Île à la Crosse in 1874. This onion skin drawing was done by Sara Riel, during her time working in the community with the Sisters of Charity, Order of Grey Nuns. Sara was a sister of the Métis leader and politician, Louis Riel.

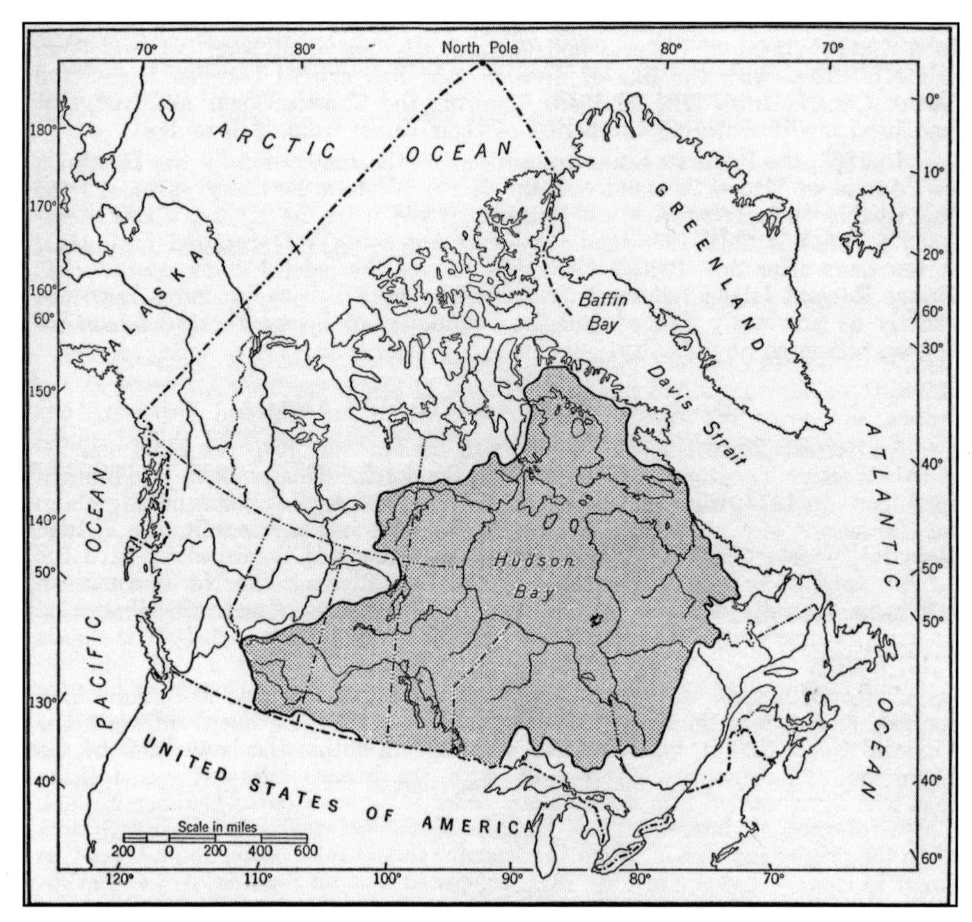

Rupert's Land, awarded to the Hudson's Bay Company by English Royal Charter in 1670, consisted of all land drained by rivers flowing into Hudson Bay. This mid-nineteenth century map by the Arrowsmith Firm shows this territory less the North Dakota portion of the Red River Valley awarded to the United States by treaty. Reporting on the character and potential of the prairie portion of Rupert's Land was the principle task given Palliser and his associates in 1857. This map owed much to the earlier cartographic work of David Thompson.

2

Canada Comes to Saskatchewan

The 1850s brought many changes to the old prairie economy, most evident in the Hudson's Bay Company's decline in prestige and social power. That the old order was disappearing was evidenced by three parallel events. The first was the mounting of a British-financed reconnaissance of prairie resources led by Captain Palliser and his associates in 1857. The second was the publication, in the same year, of a British Royal Commission of Enquiry into the affairs of the venerable old fur company. Finally, for generations of Native peoples on the prairies, it was a decade in which it was increasingly evident that the ancient 'staff of life,' the bison, were disappearing at an alarming pace.

These events were not unconnected. Palliser was selected based on his previous knowledge gained as a member of 'gentlemen' hunting expeditions on the Great Plains in the 1840s. He did not need to be told that the bison were disappearing. The old trading company, on the other hand, needed some persuading that it should give up its long-held imperial fief of Rupert's Land. The steady westward expansion of the agricultural frontier south of the 49th parallel, along with the tensions caused by the raging American Civil War, together worked to increase the frequency of political discussions in faraway cities. These increasingly tended towards a grand British Imperial gesture in favour of a new place called 'Canada.'

The negotiators were aware of the war to the south, but there was more talk about agriculture and trade. The assumption was that the future of the west, on the grasslands at least, would not be led by fur traders or be capable of supporting nomadic ways of life.

With the passage of the British North America Act of 1867 a country of uncertain health was born. After some haggling in 1869, Rupert's Land was reassigned by the British Parliament as unorganized territory to the new federal government in Ottawa. A road block on this supposed smooth path to the future was erected by Louis Riel in Red River. Somewhat unexpectedly, in 1870 'the postage-stamp province' of Manitoba became the fifth colonial unit to sign onto Confederation, on terms partially of its own making.

The northwest lands beyond Manitoba would not be unorganized for long, for at the very outset, railway enterprise figured strongly in the new political plans. Shortly after Confederation, Prime Minister John A. Macdonald and his talented civil engineer, Sandford Fleming, commenced making plans for a railway route across the west. These plans were of the greatest interest to the citizens of a fledgling mission community on the North Saskatchewan River known as Prince Albert, for in time it became known that the railway was intended to pass through this small community. As a result, financial hopes ran high in the North Saskatchewan country in the 1870s. These hopes were dashed in late 1881 when news filtered in that the Canadian Pacific Railway would no longer follow the proposed Yellowhead route from Selkirk, Manitoba to Edmonton, but would instead pass through Winnipeg and take a more southerly route across the prairies. This was good news for Regina and Calgary and bad news for Prince Albert and Edmonton.

Old overland routes such as the Carleton Trail would have to suffice for some time longer. This 'time longer' ended in 1891 when a railway branch line was completed from Regina to Prince Albert. The implications were clear enough for many of the Cree living to the north. The Lac la Ronge and Montreal Lake Bands had already collaborated a year earlier in signing an adhesion to Treaty Six in order to help ward off any potential invasion of their traditional lands. To be sure, many of those living on the new Montreal Lake Reserve were recent arrivals, having come from the Grand Rapids area near the mouth of the Saskatchewan River where organized Euro-Canadian commercial exploitation of the traditional fishery had increased.

The Hudson's Bay Company was no longer the main landlord in the northwest, but it was still alive and well and maintained a number of posts between the North Saskatchewan and Churchill Rivers including one at the Narrows on Red Deer Lake, now renamed Waskesiu Lake. The railway line from Regina was good news for the old firm, for it now had reason to build an overland route from Prince Albert to Montreal Lake, not only to serve the residents of the newly surveyed Indian Reserve, but also to develop a depot for supplying its posts on the upper Churchill River. The logic of the moment led the Hudson's

Bay Company to close the post it had established on Red Deer Lake in 1886 in favour of a new one at Montreal Lake. This new supply road to Montreal Lake followed the Spruce River and went by Shady Lake, just south of the present town of Waskesiu, before branching to the northeast. The developing community at the Narrows was thereby eclipsed.

Clifford Sifton (1861-1929). Sifton was the ambitious Minister of the Canadian Department of the Interior between 1896 and 1904. He oversaw immigration policy at a crucial time of western Canadian agricultural settlement. Sifton advertised in Western and Eastern Europe where many were anxious to take up land on the favourable terms offered by the Canadian Government.

In 1891 the federal Conservative Party had to deal with the death of its legendary leader, Sir John A. Macdonald. His much promoted economic National Policy, pursued in the interest of continent-wide nation building, had become mired in recession. The financial climate, however, had improved when the Liberals came to power in 1896 and they did not hesitate to make use of what had been achieved by previous Conservative governments. Important were the ambitious settlement programs of Clifford Sifton of Brandon, the new Minister of the Interior. He advertised western opportunities in 'The Last Best West' to the land hungry populations of the British Isles and Europe and soon the prairies were filling up with immigrant farmers. They were directed mainly to the newly-surveyed farming lands south of the forest belt. If there was still industrial depression in Eastern Canada, at least the grain economy was taking off, and with it, demands for construction materials to build new western cities.

The coming of the railway to Prince Albert in 1891 had opened up many economic possibilities in the north woods. The solid opportunities were not in the old fur trade but in fish, lumber, and perhaps minerals. The lumber industry was fast to take flight. North of the Saskatchewan River, fur traders had pioneered crude access routes to Green Lake, Montreal Lake and Lac la Ronge. These old trails were suddenly in demand as winter freight routes. They would eventually become the basis of modern highways. The so-called 'Forks' at the north end of Shady Lake became the main stopover and supply depot for lumber camps as well as the meeting point for trails to the east, west, north and south. From small timber harvests in 1880 the local sector grew until by 1910 Prince Albert mills were responsible for a sizable amount of western Canadian production – demand driven by the general post-1896 boom in construction that was taking place all across the prairie provinces.

These same old freight trails were also important in the development of another local industry – commercial fishing. Gill net fisheries developed on the basis of license permits from the Department of the Interior and many of the lakes now in the Park, such as Big Trout (Crean) and Little Trout (Kingsmere) were highly favoured by those prosecuting the new industry. By 1900 whitefish and trout were important staples in a growing regional market. Distance from markets would keep the possibilities of the Northern Saskatchewan fishery limited, but for many years it would continue to be important to the region's food supply.

After 1912, when the Great Northern Railway reached Big River west of today's park, the Waskesiu community became a more important centre of the fishery than the city of Prince Albert, and one more source of frustration to local Native bands seeking to carry on a subsistence way of life. Something of the way the commercial fishery was worked in the 1920s may be learned from the interesting diary left by Elizabeth Pease. She and her husband George were two of Waskesiu's earliest and most prominent settlers, closely attached to the Waite Fishing Company at Big River.

The fur trade itself was far from dead, although its legal conditions of operation had changed radically since Confederation. In 1900 the Hudson's Bay Company was not the only fur trading firm around. The long established French firm of Revillon Frères, founded in 1723, made a decision to enter the fur trade at a more competitive level by going right to ground and eliminating many of the intermediate wholesale suppliers from whom it normally purchased raw furs. The Hudson's Bay Company was accustomed to dealing with independent traders, but it had been many years since it had to go head-to-head with a well organized firm out in the field. Revillon opened an office in Edmonton in 1899 and another at Prince Albert in 1901. The firm erected a short-lived post at the Narrows of Red Deer Lake, then abandoned it in favour of Montreal Lake. Revillon had its best success in the Arctic but in Saskatchewan and the old Keewatin District it made its presence felt at Lac la Ronge, Île à la Crosse, Stanley and Windy River among other places. In 1908, a young adventurer, Harold Kemp, keen to make real his childhood fantasies derived from exposure to the novels of Robert Ballantyne, entered the trade and over the next 20 years would get to know the ways of both firms.

Loggers north of Prince Albert, c. 1905. This rare postcard provides a remarkable view of loggers at dusk in the winter woods north of Prince Albert.

Today one may experience something of the way the old fur routes influenced future patterns of travel by visiting Mud Creek near Shady Lake and following the Old Freight Hiking Trail which runs along the Spruce River between Highway 263 and Amiskowan Lake. The location is a historic demonstration of the evolution of these routes from ancient to modern.*

Green Lake, c. 1908. The children of Mr. and Mrs. Edward Beatty, photographed by Frank Crean. Beatty was the clerk for the Hudson's Bay Company store at this historic meeting place of the old fur trade, northwest of the Park.

*See Shanna D. Frith, *Trail Guide: Prince Albert National Park*, (Waskesiu Lake: Friends of Prince Albert National Park, 1997) pp. 32-34

3

The New North: Politicians and a Park

In 1905 the federal Liberals under Wilfrid Laurier were again triumphant at the polls. In the still powerful Department of the Interior, a new and equally ambitious man took over the reigns from Clifford Sifton: the seasoned pioneer and journalist from Edmonton, Frank Oliver. If there were some new arrangements to be made, owing to the establishment of the provinces of Alberta and Saskatchewan that same year, the land and resource base was still controlled by Ottawa and would continue to be so until 1930. For prairie citizens it meant that on many matters of natural resource exploitation, it would be business as usual with the federal government. The upside was that Minister Oliver, like Sifton before him, was one of their own. Under Oliver, however, it was not just agriculture that was seen to be important; the future was seen to lie also in forestry, fishing and mining enterprise. Under Oliver's watch the prairie provinces would be seen as much more than wheat fields. During this transition of ministerial leadership, one thing did not change. The assistant to Sifton had been young James Harkin, formerly a journalist in Montreal. He remained to serve Oliver in the same capacity. More would be heard from this man in connection with the National Parks of Canada.

J.B. Harkin (1875-1955). In 1909, Harkin, a journalist and former assistant to both Clifford Sifton and his successor, Frank Oliver, was appointed as the Commissioner of the new Dominion Parks Branch. He was a creative and forceful personality and acted in this capacity until 1936 when the Department of the Interior was dismantled and its functions distributed among several new departments.

The town of Prince Albert and its northern hinterland were now on the verge of interesting times for there were diverse views on what constituted the best use of the land. In one camp were those who thought primary resources were always worth the effort. Another camp thought that the limits of the agricultural frontier were far from reached and what was good for the south would be good for the north. Few people knew much about the reality except the scattered groups of First Nations and a few veteran fur traders of the north country, some of whom had been able to make local patches of soil near their posts blossom in the short growing season. Around the town of Prince Albert sentiment by and large favoured making use of the lands to the north for timber, fish and minerals. There were questions to be answered nevertheless, and so in 1907 the veteran Saskatchewan politician, Senator Thomas O. Davis, headed up a special committee of enquiry into the prospects of the northern portions of the province. The upshot was that the Department of the Interior dispatched Frank Crean into the territory north of Prince Albert in 1908 for purposes of inventorying the land and its capacities. Over the next two years his party travelled far and wide, eventually producing two published reports. The photographic record of the expedition provides a valuable account of that long hidden land and the small communities sustained within.*

Crean was a strong advocate of the optimistic view that mixed agriculture in much of the territory could be an important part of the future. He was inspired by those he had met such as the Métis Louis Lavallée, who worked for Revillon Frères and lived on the edge of the lake which now bears his name at the northern edge of the Park. Lavallée lived off the land but it was the quality of his local garden that intrigued Crean. Shortly after these expeditions, Arthur St. Cyr was sent into the Park area charged with surveying base lines. He was less impressed with the potential agricultural value of the land but took time to rename Big Trout Lake, Crean Lake – no doubt, one of the many names for this fine body of water over the centuries.

Crean's survey work took place at a time when there were progressive forces in Ottawa attempting to lead the nation down the pathway of enlightened resource conservation and use. The Commission for Conservation was given form in 1909 by Laurier's Cabinet. In 1911 James Harkin was asked to become the Commissioner of National Parks following passage of a new act dealing with parks and forest reserves. It was not out of keeping with these new directions, then, that when the somewhat contrary land appraisals tabled by the two surveyors working north of Prince Albert were reviewed, the Department of

* See Bill Waiser, *The New North West: The Photographs of the Frank Crean Expedition*. (Saskatoon: Fifth House Publishers, 1992).

Lavallée Lake, c. 1930. One of the earliest known residents in the Park area was a Métis from the Cypress Hills area, Louis Lavallée, who settled before 1885. He is shown here with his grandson at his cabin on the lake which bears his name on the northern boundary of the Park.

Louis Lavallée repairing a canoe by his cabin, c. 1930.

Mary Lavallée at the family cabin, Lavallée Lake, c. 1930.

the Interior sponsored yet a third reconnaissance in 1912, led this time by a forester, C.H. Morse. His report, along with one on soil and water from the hand of L. Stevenson, led to establishment of the Sturgeon River Forest Reserve in 1913.

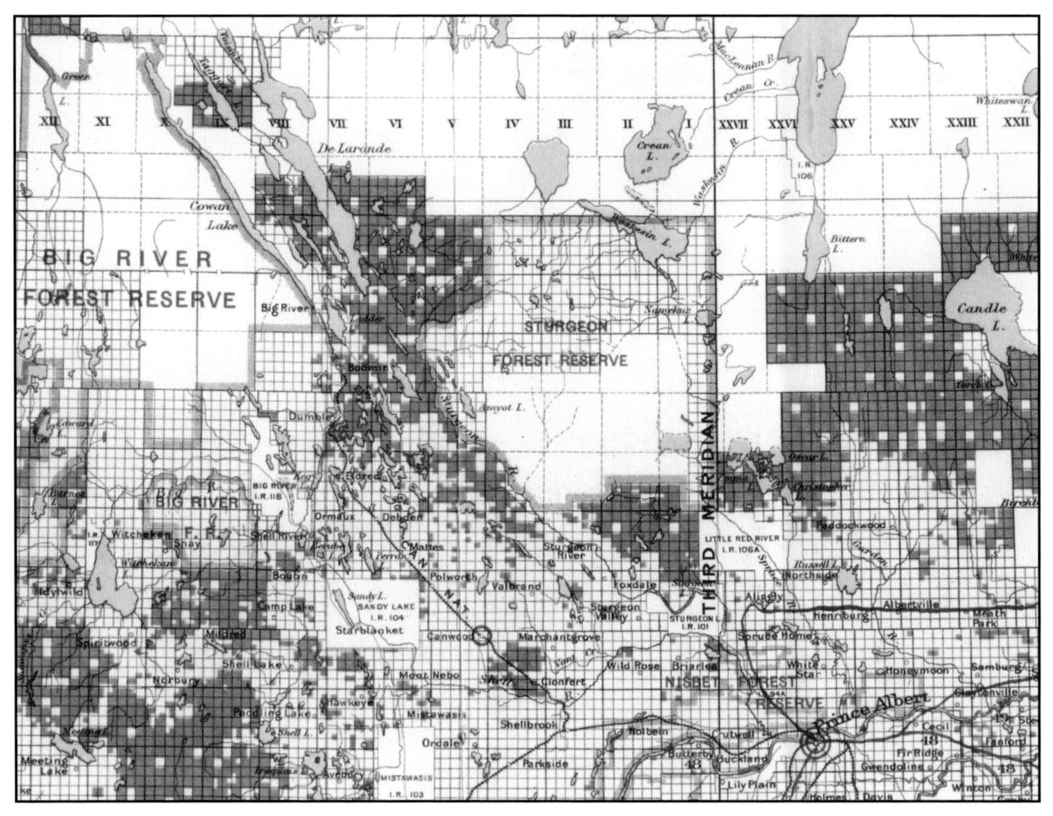

Sturgeon River Forest Reserve, 1924. After 1911 the Department of the Interior initiated establishment of several additional forest reserves under revised legislation which also allowed for the establishment of national parks. The Sturgeon River Forest Reserve was passed into law in 1913.

A number of timber limits within this new forest reserve had been active for many years, although the knowledge of a forest industry in Saskatchewan remained obscure to outsiders. When the Kennedy brothers journeyed west from Ontario in 1910 to take part in that most popular adventure of the day for young men, the 'harvest excursion,' they learned to their surprise that there was also logging going on north of Prince Albert. After checking into the Prince Albert Hotel, the main venue for the lumberjacks at the time, they were hired on the next day. In 1966, Allen Kennedy recalled how for $35 dollars per month, they were sent north to Shoal Creek 'where the buffalo park in Waskesiu National Park is now

Cree gathering, Montreal Lake area, 1920s. The early 20th century settler and fisherman of Waskesiu, George Pease, took this photograph sometime between 1915 and 1930.

located,' then the headquarters of the Prince Albert Lumber Company. He was referring to the now closed buffalo paddock area which was located near the old Park entrance on the road to Christopher Lake.

The timber firms were not adversely affected by the designation of a forest reserve in 1913. The First World War stimulated much demand for lumber and the 'timber berths' in the new reserve were harvested mainly by the company for which young Kennedy worked. In these active lumbering years water levels were manipulated by the addition of several dams on local rivers in order to ease the movement of logs. An extensive fire in 1919 however, led to the closing of the doors of the Prince Albert Lumber Company and its relocation to Manitoba. The forest reserve included much of the land in today's national park; its boundaries would later be significant with respect to the Park's establishment in 1927, allowing the federal government to continue to set some of the terms for those undertaking the prosecution of the local fur, fish and forest industries.

'Buffalomania:' first ideas for a park in the Prince Albert area.

The end of the 'Great War' provided an opportunity for citizens to think about happier prospects including recreational lands. For local community boosters in the City of Prince Albert, the forest reserve lands were not their first preference as a location for a new national park. Aware of the appeal of 'buffalo' herds as public displays at the parks in Banff, Elk Island and Wainwright, members of the Prince Albert Board of Trade adopted the view that other places might be appropriate to further this conservation effort. A proposal was hatched for Saskatchewan. Board members had approached J.B. Harkin as early as 1921 with an idea for the Pine Forest Reserve southwest of the city. Over the next five years this

Masonic Temple in the City of Prince Albert, built in 1910. This building hosted many meetings of the local Liberal Party in the 1920s. Here Thomas C. Davis, John W. Sanderson, and many others, broached ideas for a national park for Saskatchewan.

request, and similar ones from Saskatoon, were turned down. The Interior Department's assessment of the Pine Forest Reserve determined that it was not suitable habitat for bison and the proposal was put aside.

Thomas C. Davis. (1889-1961). Son of Prince Albert businessman and politician, Thomas O. Davis, T.C. Davis served as Mayor of Prince Albert and was then active as a Member of both the Saskatchewan Legislature and the Canadian House of Commons. He also served as the Canadian Ambassador to China. He was instrumental in the establishment of the Park. This picture was painted by the Russian-Canadian artist, Nicholas de Grandmaison, famous for his many portraits of Native North Americans.

When staff of the Dominion Forestry Branch approved a new cottage subdivision on Red Deer (Waskesiu) Lake in 1925, members of the Board of Trade turned their eyes northward. Road links with that area had been in place for some years and so the Board revived its interest in a new national park through the initiative of T.C. Davis, son of Senator T.O. Davis. An approach was again made to the National Parks Branch. Harkin cautioned that his department had certain criteria for national park selection and that these would have to be considered, but that he would gladly entertain a proposal. In late 1925, Davis' committee submitted suggestions for lands extending 42 miles to each side of Red Deer Lake. The plan acknowledged hopes that aspects of the buffalo park idea might again be entertained as part of the concept.

It was into this fluctuating set of circumstances that the larger political contingencies of the day suddenly thrust none other than MacKenzie King, the Canadian Prime Minister. Prince Albert's agitation for parks and bison herds was taking place at the same time that King's political career was taking a number of critical turns, initially brought on by the whiff of scandal. As is so often the case in Canadian politics, alcohol was involved, although the abstemious Prime Minister was not close to the hijinks going on in the Federal Customs Office. With prohibition raging south of the border it was not unexpected, perhaps, that the temptation for windfall profits were not always resisted by those in certain places of influence. Historian John Thompson has observed that one Joseph Bisaillon, Chief Preventative Officer of the Montreal customs district, was in fact Canada's leading smuggler – 'a protectionist by day and a free trader by night.' If King was not close to this corruption, he at least appears to have been aware of it.

In 1936, 'buffalo' eventually did find a home in the new Prince Albert National Park. At first a display herd, bison are now free ranging, as in this 1981 photo.

With these unsavoury matters under investigation, King made an uncharacteristic error. Contrary to advice offered him by his colleagues, he called an election in 1925. When the votes were counted the Liberals had lost many seats and the Prime Minister had lost his own Toronto riding. In the carnage, eight of his cabinet ministers had gone down to defeat. The Conservative Party, under the brilliant but austere Arthur Meighen, had won more seats but not enough to command a majority owing to the number of Progressive Party members returned to the House of Commons. King had to quickly find a personal solution and in November he was relieved to get information from Saskatchewan's Premier, Jimmy Gardiner, that the Liberal MP for Prince Albert, Charles McDonald, was prepared to step aside and allow King to run for the seat in a by-election. This quickly brought King to Prince Albert to meet with the riding association. In private conversations held in his train car, it is quite likely that the idea of a new national park came up. By February 1926, King found himself representing the good citizens of Prince Albert. It was surely a good omen, he thought, for had not Laurier himself once run in this riding?

4

Mackenzie King's Waskesiu

> It was evening, with the sun just vanished, there was no wind, and the lake was like glass. The only clouds were a few in the west, and these were brush strokes of crimson against an amber sky. As a background there were the dark, spruce-tufted hills of the south shore; the village flickering with beacons from outside cooking-places.
>
> - H.S.M. Kemp on Montreal Lake, 1927

In 1927, the Canadian Department of the Interior published a little book called *Vacations in Canada*. In a chapter on Saskatchewan no mention was made of Prince Albert National Park or even its prospect. Northern Saskatchewan was described rather generally 'as a network of lakes and rivers' offering 'canoe trips of the more strenuous kind.' The tourist had to go through the area 'entirely by canoe' experiencing the 'well travelled routes connecting the trading posts and missions.' One might encounter 'the charm of unspoiled country with the romance of the early days of the fur trade.' That a new national park in the middle of this territory would be on the books the following year is perhaps suggestive of just how quickly governments can move when the occasion warrants.

If the fur trade business had greatly changed in status over the last half century, the industry itself was by no means a thing of the past. There were still relatively few well-organized companies, as before 1870, but compared with the free-wheeling days of earlier centuries, there were in fact many more people in the trade in the twentieth century than ever before. Adventurous men were tempted to try their hand by the high fur prices offered for raw fur during the First World War. Just as many dropped out after the price crash in 1921, but nevertheless the Province of Saskatchewan issued no fewer than 7,500 trappers' licenses in 1924. Compared with the early days of the fur trade, it amounted to a serious invasion of First Nation's traditional lands and had dire economic consequences only partially resolved in the Treaty Land Entitlement Agreement of 1992. While the Department of Interior's vacation booklet had said nothing of a new park, rumours of it had certainly penetrated the ears of far-flung fur traders in the bush, men such as John Brooks and Harold Kemp.

H.S.M. Kemp (1892 - c. 1970). Born in Woolwich England, Kemp came to Canada in 1915 and worked as a bank clerk in Prince Albert, a fur trader, a homesteader and civil servant. His account of his fur trade days includes memorable passages about life in northern Saskatchewan in the early twentieth century.

In the spring of 1927 trader Kemp took the decision to relocate his family south from his most recent posting at Stanley Mission on Lac la Ronge. He had started out with the Hudson's Bay Company, had a brief fling with the up-start firm of Lampson and Hubbard, and was now working for the Revillon Frères Company. His children were of such an age that he wanted to give them access to larger schools and so, rather reluctantly, he packed up his family and headed for 'civilization.' In an account of his many years in the north country, Kemp mentions that prior to their departure news had reached them at Stanley of plans to set aside much of the area to the south as a new national park. When the family eventually canoed into the mouth of a river at the southwest end of Montreal Lake, Kemp knew that it flowed out of Red Deer Lake. This was unfamiliar country even to him, for he had usually approached Montreal Lake from the south by overland trail. Because of the reported newly elevated status of this terrain, he and his family gave it their 'jaundiced attention.' The lake itself 'was just another lake; we had seen scores like it.' True, 'there were some nice sandy beaches and enough trees. But it was seventy-five miles from civilization' and in addition 'behind that fringe of nice timber there was large and healthy muskeg.' The group consensus was that 'if anyone didn't mind mosquitoes after a long bush drive, Red Deer Lake might do him all right.'

Alan Nunn, the Hudson's Bay Company Manager at La Ronge, stands on the left in this 1920 photo. He is with two freightmen, employees of R. D. Brookes of Prince Albert, whose company supplied posts in the north country with essential goods. Nunn later served with Revillon Frères.

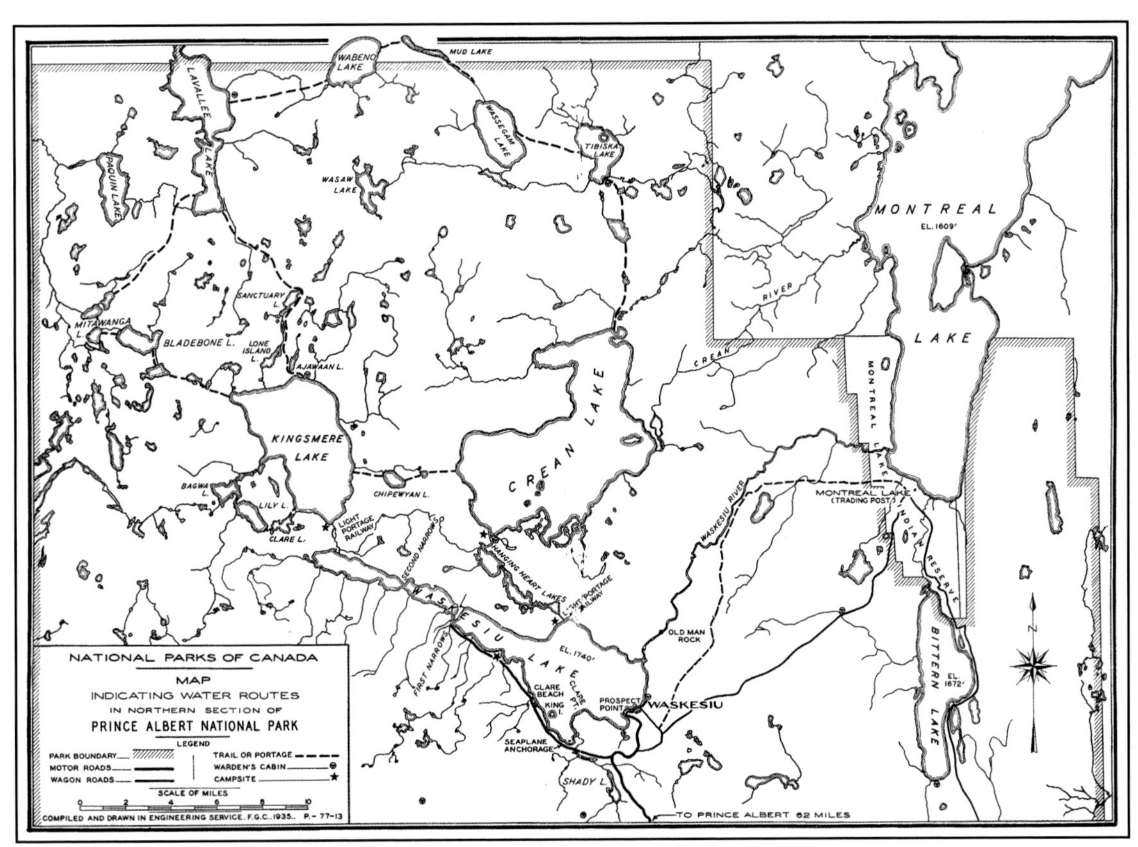

Prince Albert National Park. 1930. The original boundaries of the Park were extended two years after establishment. The northern and northwest boundary was extended north to the position in place today. More changes on the east would be made in 1947.

In that same year, somewhat more enthusiastic accounts of the country are contained in many passages in the diary of Elizabeth Pease. Accompanying her husband north of Waskesiu Lake during the fall fishery, and at one of their backcountry cabins, she wrote: 'Yesterday, I sat out of doors all afternoon and the sun was really hot.' She could 'see the fish playing among the reeds and a little farther away the ducks were splashing and playing in the water at the edge of the lake' and noticed that there was a 'thick carpet of leaves over the ground now, and in the woods there is the thick moss under the leaves.'*

It is unlikely that trader Kemp ever met the Commissioner of the National Parks Branch, James Harkin. If they had, they might have had some congenial conversations. Harkin was a man of somewhat romantic and mystical sensibilities, but he was also a man of public philosophical purpose and he did not like loose ends. To him, the manner of selection of the lands for Prince Albert National Park represented a 'loose end' for the proper comparative procedures for selecting something as important as a national park had not been followed. Kemp's instincts about the character of the lands and waters within the new park were not so far away from Harkin's initial reaction.

The Park, in retrospect, may be regarded as something of an accidental establishment. As in many other cases, it issued less from precise systematic land use planning decisions and more from the political circumstances of the day. The new park represented the culmination of a local promotion effort which had been underway for several years, but which had been running in a different conceptual direction, one which favoured prairie bison habitat. As it turned out, the initial interest in 'buffalo' exhibited by the Prince Albert Board of Trade was not entirely off the historical mark. Archaeologists subsequently found the remains of very ancient bison hunters on the shores of Waskesiu Lake and at several places much further to the north. Such relics would not signify the last of the bison in this area.

The politics of the day helped give birth to the Park, even if we are not sure just what transpired in those railway car conversations of 1926. The much analyzed, if rather misnamed, 'constitutional crisis' in Canadian political history, known as the 'King-Byng affair,' was in full blossom in June of 1926. In the wake of the Liberal election disaster of 1925, the liquor customs scandal had continued to ferment, so to speak. Rather than face inevitable parliamentary censure on the issue, Prime Minister King attempted to dissolve parliament before the matter reached the floor. Lord Byng, the Governor General, refused

---

*Diary of Elizabeth Pease, Oct. 17, 1927. Cited in Taylor, ed. *Waskesiu Memories*, Vol II. (1999), 169

to accept such overly convenient advice and countered with the suggestion that the Conservatives under Arthur Meighen should be given a chance to govern, if they could, rather than subject the people to another election. This was not what King wanted to hear and he resigned as leader of the House. Mr. Meighen was then asked to form a government. This he did, but his new administration served a mere three days before losing the confidence of the House. Rather remarkably, King had saved himself and in the following election, the Liberals came back to power with a majority. King had made much of the actions of Byng although Meighen contended there was no real crisis – a view generally supported by later historians. King's defeated opponent in the Prince Albert Riding, John Diefenbaker, later observed, with characteristic metaphor, that King's use of the 'alleged constitutional crisis' was 'so phoney it made Barnum look like an amateur.'

In the midst of all of this chaos in Ottawa, the Prince Albert Board of Trade started to rethink the possibilities. Having had no luck arguing for a 'Buffalo Park' some Board members now turned their attention north of the Saskatchewan River and considered the lands within the Sturgeon River Forest Reserve. T.C. Davis, by now a former Mayor of Prince Albert and currently in the Cabinet for the Province of Saskatchewan, urged King's Minister of the Interior, that a national park might profitably be established within the reserve. King wanted to please his new constituents and Minister Charles Stewart wanted to please King. Harkin's arguments that comparative landscape assessments should be conducted and that a better case could probably be made for the upper Churchill region were soon put to one side. The best Harkin could do was plead austerity to buy some time. However, the decision was out of his hands and, in mid-March of 1927, an Order in Council was passed by Cabinet establishing a new park of some 1,377 square miles (3,570 sq km) embracing lands within the forest reserve and other lands to the east and south of Montreal Lake, including Bittern Lake. Thus, until 1948, Prince Albert National Park was of a different size and shape than the 1496 square miles (3,875 sq km) it is today.

At the time of the Park's establishment, there were some crude road links and facilities to work with and in 1925 Dominion Forest Reserve officers made plans for a small cottage development at Waskesiu Lake. Harkin visited the area in the fall of 1927 in order to make the best of what he believed to be a questionable situation. After getting his feet on the ground, he warmed up somewhat to the prospects. In a communication with his superiors he stated that he had no doubt 'the main development to be expected in the Park will take the form of summer colonies along the shores of Waskesiu Lake.' Harkin and his associates agreed that the existing settlement at Primeau's Landing, today's Waskesiu townsite, was the correct one. They wished to make some major adjustments to the Forestry Branch's proposed subdivision plan however. The large central beach was reserved entirely for public access and the focus for cottage development reassigned to Prospect Point, soon known locally as 'the villa.' Subsequent decisions on local road development assured that the east edge of Lake Waskesiu would indeed become the main focus of the new park with boat and canoe access to the northern portions of the park facilitated by upgrading the old Big River trail which ran to the northwest and then up to the First Narrows.

With the park designation in place, the usual round of reviewing traditional place names was commenced by the Geographic Names Board of Canada. There is hardly a national park where controversy has not been generated by this exercise. Everybody had a different view about the legitimacy of this name or that. Red Deer Lake was given its Cree equivalent, Waskesiu. Cross Lake became Ajawaan, a name that soon became famous after the controversial conservationist, Grey Owl, took up residence there. After 1910 Big Trout Lake was renamed Crean on the suggestion of the land surveyor Arthur St. Cyr. Spruce Lake became Bagwa. James Wood, the new Park Superintendent, managed to get a change for the Heart Lakes to Hanging Heart Lakes, thereby recognizing a reputed battle between warring Native tribesmen. A good number of other more traditional Cree names replaced more recent designations.

Much progress was made on fundamental design and access during the first year after designation. The Prime Minister was on hand to dedicate the new park in August, 1928. In his public remarks Mackenzie King stated that the new park 'sets aside a typical example of that rich lake and woodland region lying in the northern part of the Province of Saskatchewan.' The local citizens' committee which had agitated so long for a park, was generous in its response to the Prime Minister. Facilitated by the actions of the local lumber baron, J.H. Sanderson, a rustic cottage at Prospect Point was presented to King for his use. The Prime Minister, in turn, recommended that it be made available to visiting dignitaries in the future. In fact, he never made use of it except on this singular occasion, preferring to stay with friends when he was visiting the Prince Albert constituency which he held until 1945. The original boundary of the Park did not remain in place long. In 1929 adjustments were made on the northern edge to include some of the excellent fishing lakes of that country, such as Lavallée.

The plan to attract summer tenants to the Prospect Point subdivision moved slowly despite the initial presence of its prestigious tenant, the Prime Minister. This slow growth was due to the costs and the short visitor season. With the stock market crash of 1929 and subsequent period of financial disruption, this development phase of the Park moved ahead

W.L.M. King at the Park Opening Ceremony, August, 1928. Left to right. T.C. Davis, Vern Johnson, J.A. Wood (crouching), Mayor Thomas Branion of Prince Albert, Prime Minister King, Harold Fraser, Charles Stewart, (behind King). The Prime Minister had just given Vern Johnson of Big River a Humane Society Award for the rescue of a woman during a blizzard. King is enjoying a humorous moment with Johnson's lead sled dog, Prince.

at a snail's pace. Nor was there much money for roads and other facilities. As the national economy worsened the need to provide work to unemployed workers eventually proved to be the key to constructing many needed park improvements in the 1930s.

W.L.M. King's cabin, Prospect Point. This cabin was presented to MacKenzie King for his future use at the time of the opening of the Park in 1928. The cabin was the result of private contributions and the organizational efforts of local lumberman, James H. Sanderson, who was connected to the local Liberal Party.

King cabin. Unidentified people gathered on the porch of the Mackenzie King cabin on Prospect Point.

5

Prince Albert National Park through Depression and War

Prince Albert National Park had been established on the eve of one of North America's worst periods of economic depression. Usually the first order of business for any new park involves putting in place a minimum set of facilities, but this became very difficult as the implications of 1929 unfolded. The means of getting to the Park were still primitive according to the prominent local lawyer, J.W. Sanderson:

> The area now the townsite, before there was any highway, was reached over a trail. I recall going to Waskesiu in my grandfather's touring car with its roll up canvas sides which flapped in the wind. The travellers carried axes, and from time to time, it was necessary to remove downed trees. The first version of the gravelled road through the south entrance from the Andrew Lennox farm to the lake was far removed from the next version.

On the prairies in the early 1930s, urban worker distress was compounded by mounting drought conditions in the countryside. The farm economy, in many regions, suffered the double assault of low grain prices and environmental disaster.

Owing to the cautious nature of their personal investments, neither Prime Minister King nor the new leader of the Conservative Party, Calgary millionaire Richard B. Bennett, lost heavily in the stock market crash. Perhaps for that reason, King made an insensitive blunder which would come back to haunt him. Replying in the House of Commons to the Independent Labour Member from Winnipeg, J.S. Woodsworth, King stated that his administration would not give 'a single five cent piece' in relief assistance to any provincial government that was not Liberal. Bennett seized upon the statement and King and his Liberals went down to defeat in the election of 1930. The hopes were, no doubt, that the seasoned business man, Bennett, who wanted to end unemployment by 'blasting' his way back into world markets, might be the best man to lead the country.

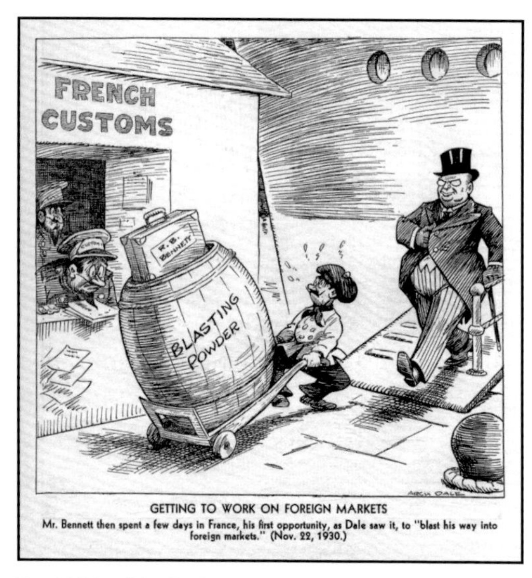

GETTING TO WORK ON FOREIGN MARKETS
Mr. Bennett then spent a few days in France, his first opportunity, as Dale saw it, to "blast his way into foreign markets." (Nov. 22, 1930.)

In 1930, this is how the *Winnipeg Free Press* cartoonist, Arch Dale, saw the new Prime Minister, Richard B. Bennett, and his promise to kick-start the economy.

One of Bennett's first moves as Prime Minister was to pass the Unemployment Relief Act. The legislation provided limited funds for provinces to finance special projects in which needed work was done for relief wages. Prince Albert National Park became a logical focus for such projects. Five camps were established from which men were dispatched to complete various tasks. At Waskesiu work focused on campground expansion. The national make-work programme was useful, but its short-term and stop-gap nature was quickly revealed as unemployment continued to burgeon across the country. New relief bills with larger budgets and expanded terms of reference became normative over the next few years. Historian Bill Waiser observed that as 'the southern part of Saskatchewan was reduced to a desert, more

Relief Workers. This photo shows employees from a relief camp at Prince Albert working on storm sewers for the Waskesiu townsite in 1935.

and more communities sent their unemployed north to the Park.' In 1932 the men 'arrived weekly in groups from 10 to 40' and by the New Year 'they surpassed 1,000.'

Superintendent Wood disliked the distraction of having to supervise all this supplementary year-round activity, but he also realized that it was probably the only way to get much needed improvements realized for the Park. For instance, a proposed new subdivision at Clare Beach west of Waskesiu was opened in 1934 despite the lack of applicants. The Bennett government was on the verge of a more Rooseveltian 'New Deal' approach to things when it passed into law the Public Works Construction Act of 1934, recognizing that more radical expenditures had to be undertaken for employment creation. As a result, the next two years saw increased funding for Prince Albert National Park and significant work was accomplished. The golf course near Prospect Point, initially surveyed in 1927, was enhanced and extended including construction of a striking rustic clubhouse. The golf course itself was much the doing of local park engineer, J.H. Atkinson, perhaps assisted by

Superintendent James Wood and family on Ajawaan Lake. c. 1932. This striking picture is also from an original black and white photo transformed into a colour glass slide. This photo may have been taken during a visit to Grey Owl's cabin.

Albert Kam. Atkinson was an enthusiastic golfer and he designed and supervised course development between 1932 and 1936. Only in 1946 did the well-known golf course architect, Stanley Thompson, arrive to play and table a report outlining suggestions.

Golf Course. 'Eratics' or 'fieldstones' of glacial origin ring the pond in this 1930s photo.

There were other achievements in the mid-1930s. The Park museum was completed in these years as a community hall. A number of other improvements were made, including picnic shelters and much needed Park staff quarters. The Prince Albert Board of Trade finally got its way on the buffalo question as well, for by the spring of 1934 a bison paddock had been completed in the southeast part of the Park. In 1936 a herd was seeded from the one at Elk Island National Park, eventually becoming a popular attraction.

During the Bennett administration the Park had accomplished much under adverse circumstances. The Conservatives had come to power at the worst possible time and they eventually took the blame for steadily worsening times and went down to defeat in the election of October, 1935. The new Liberal government, again with Mackenzie King at the helm, carried on in a similar direction as its predecessor. The townsite at Waskesiu remained the logical focus for post-1935 relief work and new work was initiated on the road system around Waskesiu Lake.

Waskesiu Clubhouse at the golf course. This fine building dates from 1934. Golfers driven in by the rain could find refuge by its large stone fireplace.

Waskesiu Clubhouse, 2007. In 1996, Edwards, Edwards, McEwen, Architects, received the Saskatchewan Architectural Heritage Society Vintage Building Award for Exterior Renovation to a Community Landmark.

By the early 1930s there were other activities aside from government initiatives. The business subdivision had been encouraged since 1927 and by 1932 a number of shops, lodges and hotels were operating, such as Ivor Frigstad's Arcade Store, completed in 1931. Now a Waskesiu institution, the Lakeview Inn was functioning as was the Pleasant Inn. There was the popular Pease Fish Shop, run by some of Waskesiu Lake's earliest settlers, and the Empire Lumber and Fuel Company, which catered to more practical needs. By 1933, however, the economic downturn was in full force. Attendance at the Park dropped radically and the 1932 level of visitation of over 27,000 would not be achieved again until 1939. The entrepreneurial spirit in the town was dampened for most of that decade.

Despite the economic disruption of the 1930s, not all at the Park was a tale of woe. These were the years of one of its most memorable personalities who became an internationally recognized promoter of wildlife conservation, Archibald Belaney, also known as Grey Owl. An Englishman who dramatically went native, Belaney has been the source of much commentary since his death in 1938.

Two fishermen with a catch at Crean Lake in 1938. *(left)*

Campground at Waskesiu, 1930s. *(top right)*

Wharf area and boats at Waskesiu Lake, 1930s. *(bottom right)*

Museum. This handsome structure was another product of the relief camp building effort of the mid-1930s. It had been proposed to be more centrally located but the Superintendent thought it should have a more scenic setting and was built on higher ground overlooking Waskesiu Lake. Today it serves as the Nature Centre.

The former bandstand at Waskesiu Lake. Many a group of musicians performed in this attractive location at the height of land near the main beach.

Royal Canadian Mounted Police Quarters. Since the establishment of the Province in 1905 the RCMP has served as the police force. Their colourful uniforms made the force members a popular aspect of the tourist season at Waskesiu.

RCMP officer with cariole on Montreal Lake. c. 1940.

A shack tent, 1930. This photograph of the Howard Camp shows the characteristics of one of the early shack tents at Waskesiu. Members of the Ridley family are visiting.

Community Hall. The public function of this mid-1930s structure was a source of disagreement between the Superintendent and Ottawa. The museum aspect was ultimately built elsewhere. Musician Ian Barrie stated that the piano in the hall was an old square Steinway which had been brought from Fort Garry to Prince Albert in a covered wagon pulled by oxen.

Terrace Gardens Dance Hall under construction in 1930. Bill Schaan, a saxophone-playing manager of a local Saskatchwan Wheat Pool appears to have been the inspiration for the dance hall, joined in his enthusiasm by Ian Barrie. Eventually it was transformed into the current Assembly building, but now retains the Terrace Gardens name.

The Waskesiu Terriers in 1935 at the Terrace Gardens.

This air photo from 1981 shows the secluded setting of Grey Owl and Anahareo's cabins where they lived with the beavers during their years at Prince Albert National Park in the 1930s.

In 1930, the Director of the National Parks Branch, J.C. Campbell, became aware of the publishing activities of an Indian at Cabano, Quebec, named Grey Owl, a man reported to have recently turned from the trapping life to that of wildlife conservation. His latest wife, Anahareo, an energetic woman of Iroquoian/Mohawk background, had been urging him to abandon the trapping life. One day he found two beaver kits by one of his traps and this proved to be his deciding moment. He and Anahareo bonded with the young animals and started a beaver colony at Cabano.

Campbell approached Grey Owl with a view to making a film of his activities. Campbell proposed to J.B. Harkin that he consider finding a place for Grey Owl within the Park system, one where he could conduct his conservation experiments with the beavers. To Harkin, the time seemed correct to supplement past achievements in conservation of birds and larger mammals with that of the beaver, the emblem of the nation. Riding Mountain National Park in western Manitoba was identified initially as the place for such a beaver reintroduction programme. Accordingly, in early 1931, Grey Owl arrived to take up his new position. He soon told authorities that he thought the water levels were too low so arrangements were completed by the fall for Grey Owl and Anahareo to transfer to Prince Albert National Park. At the end of October, the couple moved into a new cabin at Ajawaan Lake, soon known as 'Beaver Lodge,' just north of the large Kingsmere Lake. By this time, his fame had started to grow, for he had already published *Men of the Last Frontier* in 1931.

The new cabin was constructed to cater to both humans and beavers. The publicity gained was all that Parks Branch officers might have wished. The cabin became a favourite destination for Park visitors, many of whom would be greeted at the shore by its unique hosts and by its semi-aquatic rodent residents. Life thereafter would get complicated for both Grey Owl and the Park officers, for as his fame grew his behaviour became more erratic. His growing celebrity on the lecture circuit in Canada and the United Kingdom put him outside the reach of his supervisors for long periods. The independent streak which had surfaced so early in life in his native England, was not compatible with the procedures expected in a large organization. Superintendent Wood liked Grey Owl and was his friend, but his patience was severely tested on occasion. The revelation of his true identity after his death in 1938 was initially front page news in Canada and England, and for a time there was a decline in support for the man and his work.

Grey Owl at Lake Ajawaan, photographed by William J. Oliver.

We need an enrichment other than material prosperity and to gain it we have only to look around at what our country has to offer.
- Grey Owl

Grey Owl and his Times

Archibald Stansfeld Belaney was born in 1888 in Hastings, England. When his father abandoned his mother, she gave him over to the care of two aunts. Archie, as he was then known, was a good student but early on he displayed a sense of solitude that would mark him, but also serve him well. An interest in the outdoors came easily for on the paternal side of the family there were lasting connections with land and wildlife. His great uncle James had written a *Treatise on Falconry* in 1841. His early reading leaned towards tales of the North American woods and Indian life. At age 17 Archie obtained the reluctant consent of his aunts to sail for Canada and in April of 1907 he disembarked at Halifax.

Following a brief stay in the Maritimes, Archie headed for the wilds of northern Ontario to the rugged Temagami country, a shield landscape of countless lakes and rivers. Here among the Ojibwa he honed his bush skills. In 1910 he married his first wife, Angele Egwuna of Bear Island. Underneath Archie was still very much an Englishman and the solitary life of the bush was not always to his liking. The forest interior was increasingly balanced with trips to Timiskaming and the pleasures of liquor and nightlife. Whatever his childhood fantasies had been, he had learned that 'a man who makes his living in the bush earns it.' Disillusioned, he abandoned his young wife and returned to England.

It was, however, too late for young Belaney to go home again, and he merely felt more estranged from the constraints of his old domestic hearth. Before a year was out he had returned to Canada, eventually establishing a trapline in the Biscotasing area of northern Ontario. With the outbreak of the First World War, the old ambiguities

Famous for his photographs of Rocky Mountain scenery, William Oliver is shown here in the Park with Anahareo and Grey Owl.

This relaxed picture of Grey Owl at Lake Ajawaan appeared in Lovat Dickson's 1939 tribute volume, *The Green Leaf.* 'Meals are taken out of doors in the summertime and are of the simplest variety.'

surfaced again. Belaney went to Digby, Nova Scotia and enlisted in the Canadian Expeditionary Force. In 1915 he sailed for France where he was wounded and then sent to England to convalesce.

These events caused Belaney to evaluate both his condition and English life. He renewed contact with his childhood sweetheart Constance Holmes and the couple married. It was ill-fated from the start, for the dreams of both were quite incompatible. After only a month Archie again packed up and returned to Biscotasing. One does not step into the same river twice. By this time the commercial assault on the mining and forest frontier of the area had started in earnest. It was not the wilderness he remembered.

Belaney's anxiety about civilization drove him to consciously withdraw back into the world of the Indians among whom he lived. Contact was minimally renewed with his Bear Island wife, Angele Enguna and he finally met his child. He consciously adopted the appearance and ways of the Ojibwa, learned the language, and took on the identity that would propel him towards fame – *Wa-Sha-Quon-Asin* (He Who Walks by Night). The persona of Grey Owl had been born. He started to pass himself off as the 'half-breed' son of a Scotsman and an Apache woman.

But his eye still wandered and when in Temagami in 1925, he met the woman we know as Anahareo. She would become his most important, but not his last, helpmate in life. Grey Owl's relationships with women were many and complicated. His time with Anahareo was spent during the years of his most famous writings and international fame as a touring lecturer. Anahareo was as free a spirit as Grey Owl and the changing circumstances of their life together helped drive the two apart in 1936. By then, his time was short. While a few knew of his true identity, it was only after his death in 1938 that the truth came out, much to the disappointment of many of his followers. With the passage of time, interest has tended to focus less on the flamboyant and deceptive life he led and more on the broader nature of his message. Like the artist Tom Thomson, he recognized the unique opportunity to see the majesty and grandeur of a particular wilderness just when it was on the verge of passing away.

Grey Owl's cabin has been conserved in the distant reaches of the park at Ajawaan Lake. A guesthouse built for Anahereo and three gravesites belonging to Grey Owl, Anahereo and their daughter, Dawn, also nestle alongside the lake. A modern day canoeist can travel the route via the Kingsmere River portage and onto Ajawaan Lake, the same path Grey Owl so often crossed on his own.

Grey Owl paddling. Photographer W.J. Oliver caught the quiet serenity of a moment on Lake Ajawaan.

Anahareo makes friends with a black bear.

Anahareo: A Parallel Life

Archie Belaney's companion between 1925 and 1936 was Gertrude Bernard (1906-1986), a Mohawk girl from the Mattawa area of Ontario, better known to the world as Anahareo. They first met at Lake Wabikon in Ontario's Temagami country. Despite the legal complications for Belaney, in 1926 they were married in a traditional ceremony by Chief Nias Papate of the Lac Simon Ojibwa, near Doucette, Quebec. The name 'Anahareo' was eventually bestowed on her by Belaney, as a gesture towards her deep roots in the Mohawk community. He appears to have modified the name of her famous great, great grandfather, Naharrenou, a well known Chief in the Oka area.

There were some striking parallels of character in the couple. Young Anahareo was as much an individualist as her famous partner. Ironically, being more accustomed to urban life, at first she had to learn bush craft from Grey Owl rather than impart such knowledge, even though she had learned a great deal that was traditional from her guardian grandmother. She was a fast learner and after living in the bush together and working the traplines, it was she who set Grey Owl on the path towards wildlife conservation. By doing so, she unwittingly initiated the start of the end of their flamboyant and romantic life together. As the persona of Grey Owl started to surface with all the attendant demands on his time she could not just sit and watch, happy as she might be for his success.

Their daughter, Dawn, was born in 1932, after the couple had relocated to Prince Albert National Park. By this time, Grey Owl's time was no longer his own or hers. It was not the domestic life she wanted or remembered in the early years. In old age, she remarked that when Grey Owl was busy writing 'it was like living with a zombie.' Her capacity for the solitary life was well developed, but it had to be mixed with some action. She was fascinated by the life of prospecting and while Belaney was honing his skills as a writer, she teamed up with acquaintances in late 1929 for an extended trip into Northern Quebec. It would not be the last time she headed out on her own. It was an early symptom of a growing remoteness between the couple and in the summer of 1936 they parted.

For Anahareo it marked a second beginning. In 1939 she married a Swedish Count, Erik Moltke Huitfeldt, active in the construction business in the Calgary area. Following his death in 1963, she relocated to Victoria and then Kamloops to be closer to her daughters. Her autobiographies of 1940 and 1972 detailed much of interest from her own point of view. As she grew older Anahereo set her own mark upon conservation. By 1972 she was involved with the Association for the Protection of Fur Bearing Animals, particularly on the question of leg-hold traps and the use of poisons. On the basis of a nomination made by Grant MacEwan, the Paris-based International League of Animal Rights awarded her the rarely granted membership in the Order of Nature in 1979. In 1983, the Canadian Governor General, Edward Schreyer, inducted her into the Order of Canada.

Anahareo and Dawn, 1937. Anahareo's love of the canoe is shown in this photo from her first autobiography. It would be one of the last times she took her daughter paddling on Lake Ajawaan.

Anahareo as Traveller and Prospector

When the walls closed in around Anahareo, she knew what to do: head for the hills. Just how much she knew about geology is not certain, but her early progress towards tom-boyism clearly worked in her favour. In 1930 an extended period prospecting in the bush in the Lac Mistassini country with the Algonkian Dave Whitestone (Pilon) must have taught her much of the technique. At Lake Opemiska she claims they missed a fortune by being out-staked by 28 days. In 1934 she was again restless and after a call from a prospector she set off for the Chapleau country. This was unproductive but a series of other calls were received, including an offer to work at Great Bear Lake. After many visits to offices in southern Ontario and Buffalo, New York, she returned to Ajawaan to discuss matters with Grey Owl, but the finances could not be found for any of these expeditions. She then planned another trip and headed, almost casually, into some of Canada's most obscure territory on another prospecting venture. Her destination was the *terra incognita* of far northern Saskatchewan, to remote Wollaston Lake, and then to Flin Flon and finally back to Waskesiu. By the time she returned, she had been gone almost a year, with Dawn left in the care of friends in Prince Albert.

Cover of Anahareo's *My Life With Grey Owl*, 1940. Anahareo published a second autobiography in 1972, *Devil in Deerskins*.

The account of this trip that Anahareo has left us in *Devil in Deerskins*, reinforces what she had suggested in her earlier autobiography, that she and Grey Owl were both loners with a need to follow their own paths. They were close to a natural embodiment of what the poet Rilke held up in his famous image of lovers and friends as composing 'two solitudes.' In what is almost a paraphrase of the poet, Anahareo wrote in 1940:

> All the suffering and hardship my body has gone through, the weariness of the trail, the loneliness and hunger I have known through these years, might never have been. But I should have missed the things I have learnt to love: the open fire before which Archie and I sat night after night through so many winters, two lonely and hungry human specks in an immensity of forest, touching each other for security.

Anahareo, age 74, at Kamloops, British Columbia, taken by the well-known photographer, James La Bounty. Late in life, Anahareo received recognition for her own conservation efforts.

In the 1930s, photographers and filmmakers such as Charles Cowles and Myrtle Strangways were active in the Park. There is something prophetic in this calendar photo of five women on their own, displayed for the month of August, 1939. Many men would soon leave for the war in Europe. Myrtle Strangways is shown here in the car with her camera.

The literary talent of Grey Owl was not the only manifestation of the arts in this region. The Park had done much to stimulate interest in landscape painting in the community. In the same year that the Park was established, Augustus Kenderdine arrived in Saskatoon and began to explore northern Saskatchewan. He purchased a cottage at Emma Lake in the early 1930s, just a short distance southeast of the Park. After 1936, under the sponsorship of the President of the University of Saskatchewan, W.C. Murray, this property became the focus for a summer colony for artists where 'workshops' attracted many talents including Ernest Lindner, Reta Cowley, Wynona Mulcaster, and Roland Keevill, to name just a few. From its beginning on Murray Point the school has continued to develop and exert an important influence on the arts well beyond the borders of Saskatchewan.

The year 1938 in Waskesiu, as in many places, was a stressful one. Following so much international triumph, the sudden death and exposure of Grey Owl as a 'fraud' seemed to be the last straw, the final insult of a miserable decade. There was some good news in 1939, however; the crops returned to the prairies. For wheat, the average bushels per acre in 1939 reached 19.1, having fallen to a decade low of 6.4 in 1937. This return of good harvests was attended by much worse news on the political front: that of war in Europe. For the farmer in particular, the war was far from rewarding in strictly economic terms. Despite the rise in Canadian crop yields, the European markets for those crops steadily collapsed as one nation after another fell before the *blitzkrieg* or moved to improve its own agricultural resources in order to divert scarce funds elsewhere. Canadians were left with a large domestic oversupply. What used to be said regularly in the 1920s, that 'wheat sold itself,' could no longer be said. The war brought only one clear benefit: it put people back to work, although not in ways they might have wished.

Lakeview Drive, Waskesiu townsite, 1940s.

Shack tent row, c. 1949. This photo demonstrates how shack tents had evolved in style by the late 1940s from their more basic style of the 1930s.

At Prince Albert National Park the war had a contrary effect. Able-bodied men were suddenly in short supply. The new superintendent, Herbert Knight, an experienced man from Waterton Lakes National Park in Alberta, had to rely upon the labour provided by conscientious objectors who were being confined in park camps. Many others from Saskatchewan joined the active forces and the landlocked province was represented at sea by the frigate *H.M.C.S. Waskesiu* launched from Esquimalt in 1943. Park work accomplished during the war years was primarily basic maintenance.

However there was work of a very different order being conducted. The extension of the boundaries north in 1929 had brought some important conservation lands into the Park. In 1938 Ben Ferrier visited the rare colonies of white pelicans and cormorants at Lavallée Lake. The well known federal wildlife biologist, J. Dewey Soper, followed up with another inspection in 1940, guided by Warden Shorty Harrison, thus commencing the documentation of this important set of breeding populations which now enjoy legal protection by means of a 'no go, no fly zone.' The majestic pelicans annually migrate from Canada to Mexico and the Southwestern United States.

With the end of hostilities in May of 1945, visitors slowly started to return, assisted by favourable crop production on the prairies. If farm income was not all that it might be, there had at least been the return of vocational pride and the emotional buoyancy which attends the end of wartime. It was a period of renewal and initiative for the forest industry which underwent northern expansion with much attention to scientific management. Fire suppression was given a romantic tinge in 1948 when the Saskatchewan Government established the elite airborne 'Smokejumpers' headquartered at La Ronge. At Prince Albert National Park a considerable amount of catch-up had to take place in order to cater to the needs of a population stressed by years of conflict. In 1945 the Parks Branch made an effort to stimulate new cabin and bungalow sites at the Narrows, Sandy Lake and Namekus Lake, but the response from entrepreneurs was disappointing. In 1948, the Kapasiwin Bungalow development along the Heart Lake Road was authorized as another way to cater to demand. New cottage subdivisions in the townsite were opened up with enhanced standards. Most dramatic perhaps, was the rise in popularity of shack tents, by now something of an institution in Waskesiu. In the summer of 1950 there were over 400 of these unique structures in the main campground. This surge marked the onset of a trend which would lead to conflict between Park authorities and local Park users, one that would not be substantially resolved until the mid-1970s.

White pelican and black cormorant rookeries. This image shows the diorama prepared for the Royal Saskatchewan Museum by the noted naturalists, Fred Lahman and R.D. Symons, of cormorants and white pelicans in habitat reminiscent of Lavallée Lake.

The authority on birds, Percy Taverner, remarked that despite the awkwardness of the white pelicans on land, in flight they became 'a thing of grace and beauty' and that 'once they get in the air their rise is so easy and rapid that before one is aware they are circling up and up until, at times, they vanish in the blue sky.'

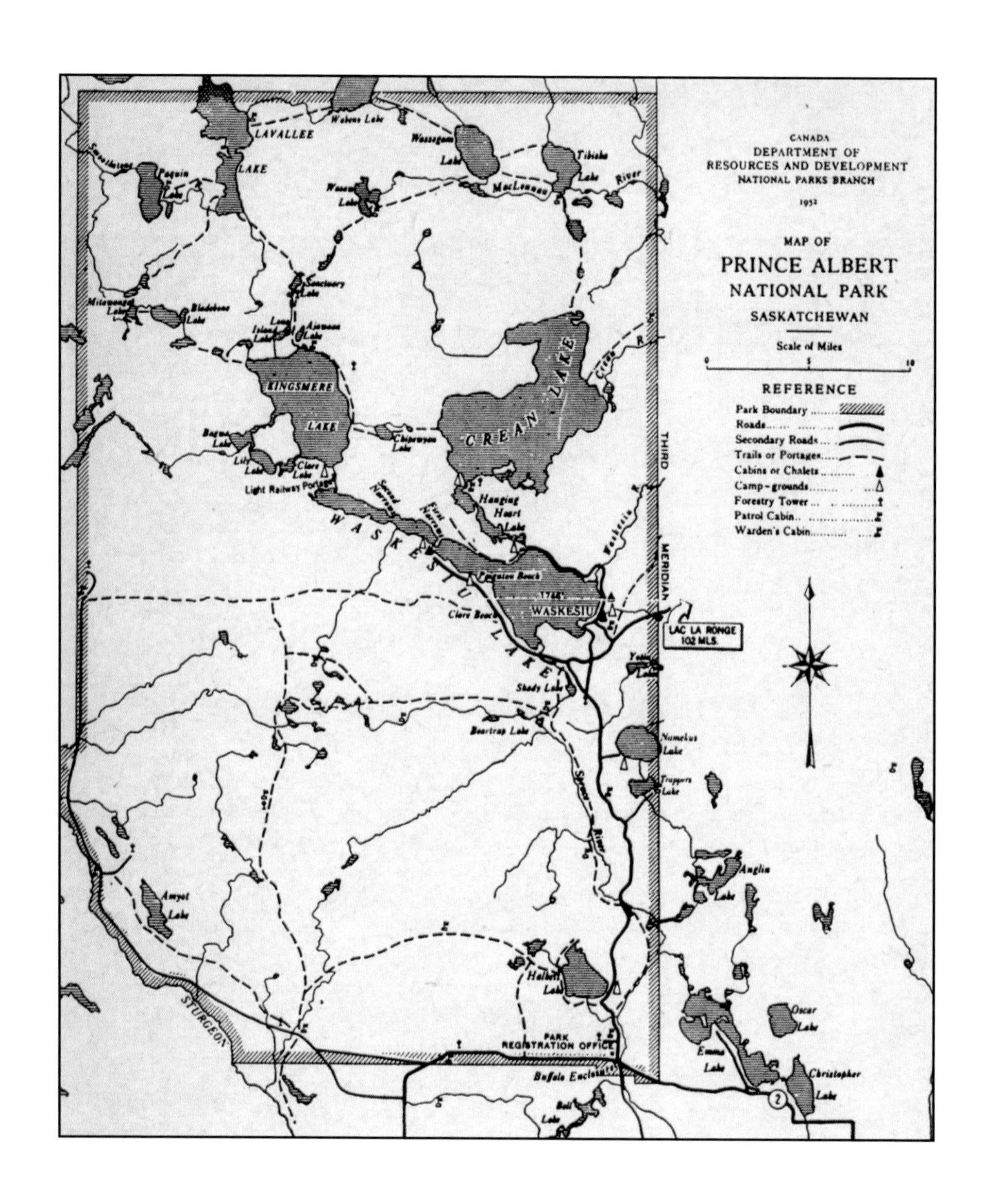
CANADA
DEPARTMENT OF
RESOURCES AND DEVELOPMENT
NATIONAL PARKS BRANCH
1952
MAP OF
PRINCE ALBERT
NATIONAL PARK
SASKATCHEWAN
Scale of Miles
0
5
10
REFERENCE
Park Boundary
Roads
Secondary Roads
Trails or Portages
Cabins or Chalets
Camp-grounds
Forestry Tower
Patrol Cabin
Warden's Cabin
LAVALLEE
LAKE
KINGSMERE
LAKE
CREAN LAKE
WASKESIU LAKE
WASKESIU
LAC LA RONGE
102 MLS.
THIRD
MERIDIAN
Tibiska
Lake
River
Wassegam
Lake
Hanging
Heart
Lake
Chipewyan
Lake
Clare
Lake
Light Railway Portage
Shady Lake
Beartrap Lake
Namekus
Lake
Trappers
Lake
Spruce
River
Anglin
Lake
Amyot
Lake
Halkett
Lake
Oscar
Lake
Emma
Lake
Christopher
Lake
Buffalo Enclosure
PARK
REGISTRATION OFFICE
STURGEON
Bell
Lake

6

Shack Tents, Evinrudes and Rock 'n Roll

During the post-war recovery years in Canada money was tight, but by 1951 the hard work was paying off. The citizenry was ready to spend a little more time relaxing, at least for a couple of weeks in the year. In urban parts of the country many middle or upper income families managed to relocate 'to the lake' for the better part of the summer. Going 'to the camp' or 'to the cottage' became an important weekend ritual. The 1950s became the great age of the motorboat, waterskiing, canoe rentals, still-fishing from rowboats and fly-fishing on lakes and streams. It was also the time of outdoor group meals, evening dances, cherry cokes, Elvis and the outdoor barbeque. If Ontarians played in Muskoka, Saskatchewanians played at Waskesiu.

The 'Big Beach' was first known as Primeau Beach in the pre-1927 Forest Reserve days. Ever since then, it has been the focus of town activities. A tourist, peering through his binoculars on a scorching summer day, viewing a beach volleyball game, hundreds of people in the water, bright umbrellas, boats, sandcastles, and bathing suits of all colours and description said: 'The place looks like Hawaii!'

The main dock area on Waskesiu Lake, the traditional pre-war meeting place, remained in high demand. It was not just the tie-up place for the long established licensed tour boats such as the *Queen*, the *Shamrock* and the *Princess*, but by an increasing number of private boat owners. On the 'Big Beach' young men worked as lifeguards and on the golf course as caddies. Others sought landscaping jobs. In the soda fountains or at the resort hotels, young women held their first jobs. Chambermaids were sought after as the older hotels were being supplemented by something newfangled called 'motels' such as the Skyline which opened in 1954. At the new Park Twin Theatre the movies changed everyday. Summer invaders could get tennis instruction or golf and swimming lessons. Lawn bowling was a great favourite. There were regular wiener and marshmallow roasts on the beach for young and old. With establishment of year-round quarters for Park staff, that most Canadian of architectural signatures, a curling rink, was added to Waskesiu in 1959. The local RCMP officers, present from the beginning of the Park, were often seen in dramatic full red, but rarely heard. Free films were shown on occasion at the community hall and the roller skating rink was always well used. In 1961, the old Saratoga Grill was converted into a laundromat, the 'Wash-ka-sou.'

Bowling at Waskesiu.

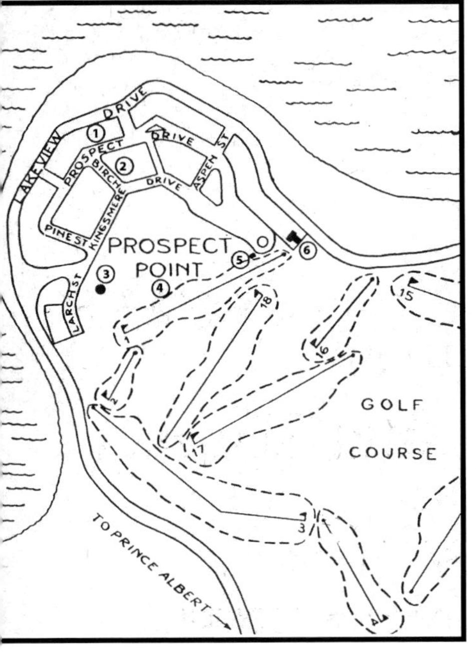

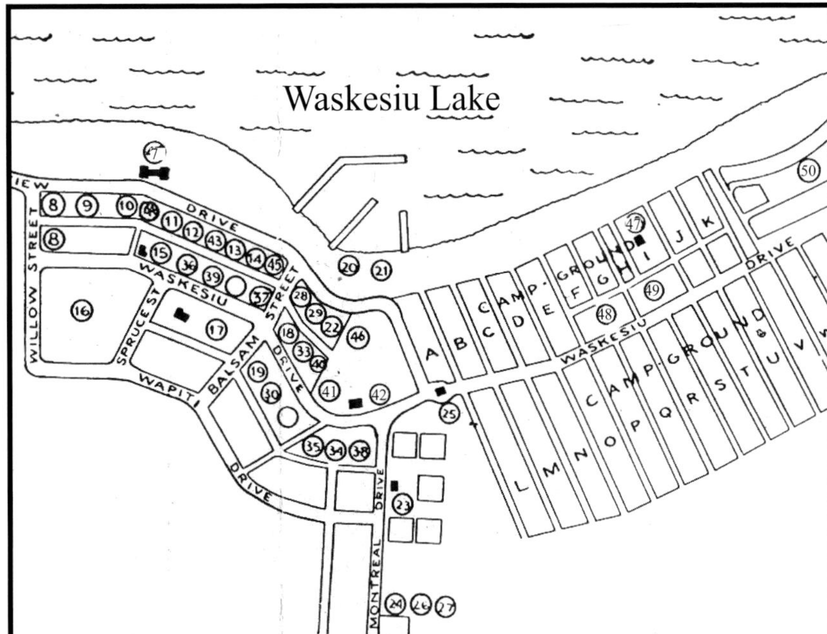

Waskesiu Townsite: 1958

Public Buildings.
Campground Office (25)
Community Hall (47)
Superintendent's Residence (1)
Museum/Nature Centre (7)
Park Administration Building (46)
Post Office (13)
Staff Quarters (42)
Telephone Exchange (Pleasant Inn) (18)

Recreation/Facilities.
Brayford Boats (21)
Golf Course (4)
Golf Caddy House (5)
Golf Club House (6)
McLaren and Grennop Boat Service (20)
Playground (49)
Skatehaven (Roller Rink) (24)
Park Twin Theatre (34)
Tennis and Bowling Clubhouse (23)
Terrace Gardens Dance Pavilion (44)
Water Tower. (3)

Accommodations.
Lakeshore Apartments (14)
Hillcrest House (8)
Hillcrest Cabins (16)
Idalodge Court (15)
Kapasiwin Bungalows (32)
(off map, right)
Lakeview Hotel (10)
Lakeview Subdivision (50)
Northland Motel (36)
Prospect Point Subdivision (2)
Pleasant Inn and Motel (18) (33)
Red Deer Chalet (12)
Skyline Motel (17)
Trailer Camp (48)
Waskesiu Bungalow Cabins (31)
(off map, right)
Waskesiu Lodge (9)

Restaurants.
Rusty's (35)
Narrows Bungalow Cabin Restaurant (42)
Lakeview Hotel Dining Room (10)
Hunter's Lunch (13)
The Coffee Shop (28)
Milk Bar (29)
Saratoga Grill (43)
Holliday Inn (30)
Waskasiu Bungalow Cabin Lunch
Counter (31) (off map, right)

General Stores.
Arcade Stores (22)
Arner's Store (35)
Lakeside Grocery (14)
Waskesiu Bungalow Cabin Store (31)
Kapasiwin Bungalow Cabin Store (32)

Specialized Stores/Services.
B.A. Waskesiu Service (38)
The Beach Comber (45)
Camera Crafts (19)
L.A.D.'s Realty (45)
Lakeview Service (Imperial) (11)
A. Leavitt. General Contracting (26)
M & K Hardware &Plumbing (39)
Pease Fish Shop (40)
Physician's Residence. (41)
Park Twin Theatre (34)
Sweeney Electric (15)
Texaco Service (37)
Waskesiu Livery (27)
Waskesiu Drug Store (22)
Waskesiu Meats (22)

At the Narrows:
Narrows Bungalow Cabins and Store

The Park Twin Theatre served a dual purpose of nightly movie entertainment and church services on Sundays.

Not all activities were secular in tone. The Park Twin Theatre would temporarily vacate its normal function in favour of a schedule of periodic praise on Sundays at 11 am. The cooperative ethic of Saskatchewan extended to denominational sharing of limited facilities. In 1958 this formal arrangement provided that on June 29th it would be the Anglicans; on July 6th came the Nazarenes; the 13th was the turn for the United; on the 20th, the Covenant; on the 27th, the Pentecostal. The Anglicans returned on August 3rd; the Baptists attended on August 10th; the Salvation Army on August 17th; the Lutherans on August 24th; and finally the Presbyterians on August 31st. The Roman Catholics held regular Mass at 12:15 pm, commencing May 18th 'and each Sunday thereafter until further advised.'

Waskesiu in the 1950s was first and foremost an operating summer town with a park attached. As such, the Park was in keeping with the original hopes of Park promoters in the 1880s, who saw parks as 'pleasuring grounds' with formal means of access and accommodation. This conformed with the conventional wisdom of developers of all types that 'if you build it, they will come.' This usually proves to be as true of townsites as it is of baseball stadiums, casinos, or roads.

In the 1880s hotels of various qualities were quickly built along the railway route through the mountains to cater to those willing to make the long trip. What has changed since those early days is the mode of access. Then it was mainly by rail and by the end of the Second World War it was mainly by motor vehicle. Until 1945 there was little reason to think that parks, as an idea, were incompatible with small service centre towns offering appropriate recreational facilities. This is certainly the message derived from any number of personal reminiscences which have come down to us from regular users of parks across the continent. Close students of group behaviour have observed that most people who go to parks do not do so to 'get away from it all' in terms of human contact. The general run of humanity proves to be just as gregarious in parks as in the city. For this reason, people tend to stay in the townsites or in group campgrounds. This easily verifiable condition has many advantages from an administrative point of view and is quite desirable from an environmental point of view. To the extent that we wish to identify parks with wilderness or 'hands off' concepts, the human tendency to cluster in groups makes it easier to define and contain conflicting land uses. The virtues of such *laissez faire* approaches to the accommodation of seasonal vacationers did not remain the conventional wisdom as the world grew more complicated in the 1960s.

In 1959 something new was blowing in the air in the far-off corridors of National Park Headquarters in Ottawa. The scent of historical error had been picked up. Planning authorities started to revisit the finer administrative detail of the parks which had made it onto the books. The appropriateness of the identity of Prince Albert National Park as 'Saskatchewan's Playground' started to raise a stir in some minds. Is this what parks should be all about? This early manifestation of environmental navel gazing came about after John Diefenbaker's attainment of power in 1957. The new Prime Minister's earlier view of the Park naturally required a certain shift in personal attitude, for after all it was now a park in *his* constituency. In earlier years he had viewed it, somewhat as had trader Kemp, as 'that mosquito park offered to Prince Albert as a reward for the election of Mackenzie King.' In 1959, Diefenbaker did not give the Park a great deal of extra thought but supported the efforts of his Minster, Walter Dinsdale, to curtail perceived private privilege in the national parks. Mr. Dinsdale had picked this idea up from national park planners who had become overly sensitive to the proliferation of shack tents in the townsite. These popular, low-cost shack tent lease sites, along with those for portable cabins were becoming a target for planners who wished to redevelop Waskesiu more in keeping with general national park guidelines. It seemed to many in the Prince Albert National Park locality that the shack tenters were being selectively targeted, leaving wealthier homeowners and traditional tenters or hotel users to carry on as usual. A summer residents' association was established as early as

John Diefenbaker fishing at Lac la Ronge after the 1957 election victory which made him Prime Minister of Canada.

1950. In 1967, under the leadership of Mary Jackson, the Waskesiu Tent Cabin and Portable Cabin Association presented a petition to Minister Laing and continued to keep the federal government's feet to the fire over what they suggested was a biased policy against the recreational habits of median and lower income users. They were asking in their own way: 'Why shoot the shack tenter?'

The controversy was far from put to rest when a Provisional Master Plan for the Park was released for public consultation in 1971. Now out of power as Prime Minister, Mr. Diefenbaker was more inclined to defend the Park and the rights of the common citizen to make use of it. In the intervening years, regional voices had successfully moved him away somewhat from the position he had taken earlier. Diefenbaker and Saskatchewan Deputy Premier, Davey Steuart, found themselves united in denouncing the current plan proposals as the misguided ideas of far-off Ottawa bureaucrats. The battle would continue for several more years until Parks Canada finally retreated in 1975 and adjusted some of its ambitions for townsite re-design.

Shack tents and portables had become more comfortable and colourful by the 1970s. These older structures are rapidly being replaced by modern, ingenious dwellings that include plumbing.

Paignton Beach. This location outside of the main townsite has always been a favourite gathering place for campfire picnics.

Chilling at Murphy's Bay on a hot summer day. This is a favourite spot to go diving for golf balls driven into the lake from the third tee box of the golf course.

Despite all this, the national parks were moving in other happier directions. In the 1960s, a significant advance in popular public education was made when various parks systems and the Canadian Wildlife Service started to introduce 'interpretative' programmes at various locations. At Prince Albert National Park this was already an old tradition to some degree, given the earlier accommodation of Grey Owl as a public relations figure for wildlife awareness, and the occasional educational efforts by park wardens and naturalists. Moe Mareschal, for instance, in recalling Boy Scout days in the Park in July of 1951, spoke of the east side of Waskesiu Lake: 'While we were there one of the Park Wardens paid us a visit and gave us a "nature afternoon" identifying trees, smaller plants, birds and animal tracks. He made a great impression on many of us and in the process nudged some of us along a path of conservation and appreciation of Nature.'* In the 1960s, young people with a good grounding in natural history were more routinely hired to take groups of visitors on short guided excursions where the hidden and not-so-hidden secrets of nature were revealed in imaginative ways. The traditional evening campfire was supplemented by talks and audiovisual productions. The Park facilitated this approach with enhanced trails and construction of pleasing and well crafted boardwalks into wetland areas. Prime Minister Trudeau was a devotee of wilderness adventure and after 1968 his various Ministers of Indian and Northern Affairs continued to advance park interpretation programmes and to expand the overall system of parks with great vigor.

There were other wildlife innovations around the Park in the late 1960s, not entirely of the Park's doing, but which had long term consequences. They would no doubt have delighted those early members of the Board of Trade who had argued long and hard for a 'buffalo park.' In 1969, 50 bison taken from the Elk Island National Park population in the Beaver Hills of Alberta were released in the Thunder Hills north of the Park in order to improve the subsistence hunt for resident Native peoples. Such experiments tend to have a life of their own. Several head drifted into the Park and over the years have migrated south to more favourable habitat in the southwest portion of the Park along the Sturgeon River Valley. This free-ranging herd now moves over a mix of private and public lands and numbers between 300 and 400 head and is one of only a few such unfenced herds in Canada.

National Park Administration has been relatively stable within the federal bureaucracy since its earliest days in the Department of the Interior. The basic value of the park system has seldom come under attack, either from the public or from politicians. After the short Conservative Administration of Joe Clark in 1979, however, the Parks Branch began a series of organizational migrations which seemed to place it on the defensive in terms

---

*Moe Mareschal, 'Boy Scouts in the Park' *Waskesiu Memories*, Vol. II. 79

of both identity and budgetary independence. In the early 1980s it no doubt made sense to consider placing the Parks Branch within the new Department of the Environment, for surely there was a natural link in the mandate of the National Parks and sound general environmental stewardship. Expectations ran high, but as Rick Searle makes clear in his free-wheeling history of the National Parks, not all was smooth sailing thereafter. However, the beginning was promising. Parks Canada released a comprehensive new policy statement in 1979, fondly known to those in the organization as 'The Beaver Book.' Some wits noticed that the stylized beaver logo looked rather more like Snoopy. This was the first important revision of guidelines since 1967. The new policies went further down the road of land-use zoning and sought to put curbs on visitor activities. The general thrust was to assure Canadians that the organization would do its best to look before it leaped and that more attention would be given to planning based on sound research and environmental assessment. The notion of 'carrying capacity,' long familiar to wildlife biologists as a way of discussing the optimum number of a given species on a given unit of land, now had a brand new direction of application: *homo sapiens canadensis touri*.

At the same time, what did it mean for the Park, when, for example, there was the awkward necessity to reaffirm in policy that 'quality visitor experiences' would be maintained. By this time, expectations had been built over many years that inter-lake travel by powerboat should be maintained. The effort by the Park to curtail access to certain sensitive lakes by special zoning was the cause of some initial conflict. The rationale provided, favouring the conservation of species was generally well-received, however.

Mike Jones practising his wolf howl at the Narrows Amphitheatre. Going out in the evening with Park Interpreters to call and listen for wolves was one of the popular events in the 1980s.

The new directions were advanced by the expanding Interpretive Programme. Park interpretive naturalists, ever an inventive lot, developed approaches for dealing with larger groups on the trail and offered inspired special events. In the late 1970s, for example, one might ask, what was it like to follow Mike Jones as he led a large auto convoy into the darkness of night? Cars filled with visitors of uncertain, but expectant mind, came to rest at the appointed place, engines and lights were cut and vehicles emptied. The people bonded cozily into a disciplined and stone-silent crowd, slowly feeling the starry night envelop young and old together. All now waited for the responses, as Jones howled for the wolves 'out there somewhere.' This was the kind of experience that provided a special kind of memory, particularly for those who had spent most of their lives in the city. At moments such as this, a sense of what later came to be called 'ecological integrity' and what an earlier generation called mystery, had a chance of registering on even the most resistant sensibility.

Road Warriors, Waskesiu Lake, 2008. While wolves are now welcome in the Park, this was not always the case in earlier years. This photo was taken by wildlife photographer Jason Leo Bantle.

Red fox are very common in the Park. This photo was used as the illustration for the cover of J. David Henry's *The Red Fox: The Catlike Canine*, published by the Smithsonian Institution in 1986.

Not all wildlife was as elusive as the wolves. Parks provide excellent opportunities for disciplined research. In 1986 David Henry published a notable ecological study of the red fox - 'the catlike canine' - a creature familiar to many Waskesiuians. According to Henry, 'their lack of shyness results from the fact that over the past half century they have not been hunted.' Initially distracted from a study of bears by these creatures, Henry then spent 14 years getting to know the red fox and allowing them to get to know him. None other than Jane Goodall called the book 'a small masterpiece.'

Under the new Environment Canada umbrella, consideration of the amount of impact that the Park could endure helped revive interest in Grey Owl once again. Not surprisingly, the well-travelled Englishman experienced rehabilitation as an icon of 'environmental awareness' and his books reappeared in paperback editions. To be sure, efforts to brighten up the tarnished image of the flamboyant impostor had started shortly after his death at the hands of his publisher. Lovat Dickson brought out *The Green Leaf* as an illustrated memorial edition in 1939 along with a full biography in the same year. Anahareo's *My Life With Grey Owl* followed in 1940. In 1988, the neglected buildings at his old home on Ajawaan Lake were refurbished after a wealthy American couple, Edwin and Margery Wilder, provided funds for restoration and for establishment of the Grey Owl Wilderness Area. His place in public memory has certainly had staying power. However, in the period between the appearance of *The Green Leaf* and the Wilder's landscape initiative, historians had caught up with the full extent of Grey Owl's strengths and weaknesses as both a person and a conservationist. The late and generous revival of his place in the Park's history by the Wilders certainly represented the triumph of affection over more earthy historical understanding.

By this time the ravages of inflation had started to take a toll on public expenditure. The developing official views in favour of resource protection lent itself well to the old spirit of 1959, that austere ethic which suggested that enjoyment, if we must have it at all, should be severely reduced as an opportunity. In the case of Prince Albert National Park, a highly representative example of a northern prairie-woodland landscape, used for centuries by diverse peoples in the course of their differing occupational seasonal rounds, was in the process of being reinvented as a pristine wilderness. Even J.B. Harkin, given his initial scepticism about the values of Prince Albert National Park, would have been hard-pressed not to open his eyes a bit wider.

Some Waskesiuians, old enough to have remembered Harkin, did open their eyes wide, and what they saw was not always to their liking. The accumulated efforts to sanitize the townsite of facilities considered inconsistent with environmental ethics were sometimes lamented by older park users. In the 1990s, Shirley Lambert observed that the 'roller rink is a magical memory. The diving board had been removed and sand is washing through the breakwater.' Furthermore, the 'canal to Heart Lakes is no more, and the paved road to the Narrows is washboard gravel. The old road to Kapasiwin next to the lake, formerly enjoyed by many for safe jogging, walking and cycling, is overgrown with brush.' Lambert regretted that 'the beaver dam with the lookouts and walkways on the Narrows Road has disappeared, and the campgrounds at the Narrows and Paignton Beach are closed.' Finally, 'the shack tents and cook kitchens are things of the past, as are the old log dressing rooms near the beach and breakwater where we so carefully carved our names on the uppermost log.'* For Lambert, and many others, the past at Waskesiu had become a foreign country.

---

*Shirley Lambert, 'The Way It Was' in; Dorell Taylor, ed. *Waskesiu Memories*, Vol. II, 75

Others were more measured in their expressions of regret about the new order. The congestion which had developed along the big beach over the years during the high season was compounded by the growth in demand for use of the original marina facility on the western side. The marina and dock were, of course, an important part of the charm of Waskesiu, as with any shoreline resort. It was not just numbers, however, but the water pollution factor which had to be addressed. Two seasoned fishermen musing about the changing times concluded that although the removal of the marina was 'a sad event' nevertheless 'perhaps in a strange way it was for the best' for the 'memories of the old marina are clear and fresh, and the new era of boats and boating is perhaps best elsewhere.'*

If the 1960s had given birth to an increased awareness of the natural environment and its fragility, the rising prosperity of North American life still continued to foster consumerism and automobile travel. Parks continued to be popular and their administrators pressured to develop new facilities. In the early 1980s, one well-known Canadian conservation group sponsored a gathering in which the central question posed was *Parks and Tourism: Progress or Prostitution?* These were tough words to use as alternatives concerning what most citizens would have considered a necessary condition of parks. The search for solutions among the newly-born environmental groups provided a wide range of answers.

Rising storm over Waskesiu Lake. Canoeists must be wary of storms which can come up rapidly on the lakes of Prince Albert National Park.

* George Whitter Jr. and Frank Poole, 'Recollections of Old Fishing Friends' in *Waskesiu Memories*, Vol. II, 194

Despite engineering guru Buckminister Fuller's pithy observations first issued in the late 1940s, the idea that there were too many people on the planet, consuming too vigorously, seemed curiously absent from many later discussions of environment. It was left to cartoonist Walter Lantz to drive the point home. In the funnies, his famous philosopher of the Okefenokee Swamp, Pogo, was made to famously quip that 'We have met the enemy and it is us!' While the economics of oil and inflation in the mid-1970s put a curb on the pace of post-war abundance and car-based recreational habits, the general attitude of working North Americans was that even if there was a bit of a temporary crisis in supply, it was still a bit early for anybody, such as myself, to take any real serious action. On the whole, most parks across North America continued to die from success. It was fitting perhaps, that just prior to the onset of the austerity of the 1990s, Bill Waiser published his history of the Park which he entitled *Saskatchewan's Playground*. As a title it summed up well what the Park had been in earlier days; but the identity of the Park as a playground would not long survive in the 1990s.

The Paddlewheeler. This was one of several tour boats which regularly plied Waskesiu Lake over the years.

7

Discovering the Limits of Fun: Waskesiu Moving Forward

As the reins of national government were passed over in 1993 from the Conservatives to the Liberals, Park enthusiasts could look back to some major achievements during the years of the Mulroney Administration. After the centennial celebrations of 1985, the 1930 National Parks Act was overhauled. In the revised act of 1988, the maintenance of 'ecological integrity' was identified as central to the mandate. The protracted and sometimes heated exchanges over what was permitted in the Park were addressed in a new Park management plan in 1987 which set in motion a process for preparation of a formal community plan and establishment of a Waskesiu Advisory Council. At Ottawa headquarters there were also many new Park proposals awaiting attention. Unfortunately, the full extent of the national financial crisis was front and centre with the new government, assisted by troublesome credit ratings generated in New York City. The vocalizations of the recently formed, Western Canada based Reform Party provided many suggested solutions, central to which were massive reductions in government expenditure. General panic set in over the extent of the national deficit. At a time when there was much desire to expand the park system into unrepresented areas of the Canadian landscape, especially in the far north, a severe national belt-tightening programme was imposed in the name of debt-reduction. All promises were off in the wake of government-wide 'programme review.'

This sudden and drastic financial austerity imposed on government spending was felt up and down the line as politicians of all stripes, federal, provincial and municipal, reshuffled their financial decks in search of ways to come to terms with the Canadian national debt. 'Downsize' and 'download' were the universal signs seen along the road to fiscal restitution posted by anyone in a position to pass costs downward to some other suffering level that could not fight back. The cartoon strip 'Dilbert' was born and became a favourite in offices across the continent with its merciless satirizing of the latest fads in management style.

The upshot for the national parks was that many services which visitors were accustomed to receive as part of their entrance fee were suddenly chopped. It was a major shift in principle from what Harkin had advocated. He had favoured the commercial provision of accommodation and basic entrance and camping fees, but concerning the larger park landscape it was 'the duty of those in charge to make them freely accessible by road and trail.' Harkin would no doubt have pursed his lips if he could have read a mid-1990s justification statement for imposition of 'user fees' beyond the basic entrance charge. Now it was stated that 'tax dollars pay for the cost of having and protecting national parks and national historic sites; those who derive additional benefit will pay to use them.' It would not have occurred to Harkin that there was a clear difference in principle. He would have agreed with many subsequent conservationists who have argued that parks and special areas are much like schools, and that all citizens benefit from them whether they use them directly or not.

Youngsters at tennis court. While issues of policy were being thrashed out, the usual summer pursuits at Waskesiu remained popular. Here youngsters are being initiated into tennis by their youthful instructor. In the background is the log Chamber of Commerce building.

The idea of 'ecological integrity' had surfaced in the 1980s and had come to inform the new National Parks Act. As a watchword of responsible environmental policy it was now necessary to put some flesh on the bones of this ambiguous doctrine. It suggested that there was a certain ideal stability in the natural environment which it should be the object of policy to maintain. This extended even to a growing respect for forest fires as agents of ecological balance. The existence of such a natural stability was, however, by no means a self-evident proposition, either on historic or scientific grounds. Since the birth of modern geology in the late 18th century, we have come to realize that there is little that is stable in the natural world. Just 12,000 years ago, a mere second in geological time, the entire extent of Prince Albert National Park had been covered by thick layers of ice, the vestiges of which are still quite visible to the modern hiker and golfer. To sort out such ideas for the public it would have been useful to engage the talents of the interpretive corps. Regrettably, given the time and effort spent in building it up over the previous three decades, this service was cut to the bone in the mid-1990s.

The Park Management Plan of 1995 dutifully soldiered on, announcing adherence to 'An Ecosystem-Based Approach to Park Management.' The statement of intent was one thing but knowing how to proceed quite another. In Prince Albert National Park, as in many other places, the spruce budworm continued its ravages on the mixed forest stands of black and white spruce and balsam fir. Here was an issue where 'ecosystem' management might be expected to shed some light, but the question of what should be done remained a delicate one for aesthetic reasons. Should park officers act locally for immediate benefits, or allow the infestation to run its natural course, as scientists might urge? On a sensitive issue such as this nobody, especially local politicians, wanted to stand on principle too rigidly. Others took to the street in protest.

The spruce budworm environmental issue. A group protest — a sign of the times.

There was another way in which 'ecological integrity' came more practically into play: the summer residential zone water supply. One veteran park user has observed that a book could be written on 'the trip to the washroom' at Waskesiu. Traditionally, it was something of a social event. People could often be heard to say: 'Guess who I ran into in my pyjamas on the way to the washroom?' With the battle about shack tents over, the late 1990s saw a beginning made on providing the dwelling areas with running water. Prior to this time everyone employed various ingenious methods of dealing with their water and washroom needs. Here was 'ecological integrity' which everybody could applaud, even if certain social traditions were thereby lost, for many a spontaneous party and coffee klatsch had been started by chance meetings on the way to the facilities. People would suddenly go missing during these ritual encounters which might commence at any hour of the day.

The concept of 'ecological integrity' was soon matched by advocates on the cultural side of the Parks Canada programme. The parallel slogans were those of 'commemorative' and 'cultural resource integrity.' As with their counterparts, these ideas were not easy to comprehend. In Prince Albert National Park, for example, dams were of several kinds, the most common the work of beavers. Those of human construction might be considered 'cultural resources' and those of the beaver persuasion might be considered natural. Beavers, when high in their cycle, proved capable of reeking great havoc in terms of flooding. Remnants of man-made dams on the other hand, dating from pre-Park times when lumbering was still in favour, had been put in place to maintain levels in streams for the transport of logs. During the First World War, it is estimated that about 125 square miles (324 sq km) in the Park area were logged. These logs were driven to the Sturgeon River en route to Prince Albert. Each 'integrity' concept could sometimes stumble over the other. After the Second World War, new dams and channels put in place to stabilize water courses between Crean and Waskesiu Lakes received mixed reviews. Two veteran sport fishermen credited these structures with inducing lakeside

Feeding moose. A familiar scene in the lakes and marshes of Prince Albert National Park.

erosion and ruining the lake trout populations. When more recent policy provided for removal of the Waskesiu River dam and replacement with a softer device known as a 'riffle', these same two men praised the decision although they were not sure that ecological restoration would necessarily ensue.* Understanding what is natural and what is artificial, in just this one single issue of water-courses suggests how cloudy pursuing goals of 'cultural' and 'ecological integrity' quickly becomes.

Veteran park naturalist and interpreter, Brad Muir, with one of his sled dogs.

If senior park officials of another generation once preferred to read the natural history classics of Thoreau or Seton they were now more likely to read Peter Drucker on management or Faith Popcorn's formulas for organizational success. Few wanted to listen to what McGill's Henry Mintzberg had to say about downsizing and the need to value accumulated knowledge and experience in large organizations. Fewer still wanted to hear the arguments of John Rohe's *Bicentennial Malthusian Essay* in which he echoed, in scholarly fashion, Pogo's dictum that the problem was 'us.' In short, Rohe argued that as an influential species we were multiplying too readily and leaders in high places were remaining massively indifferent to this issue.

Not surprisingly, the language of the 1995 Park Management Plan reflected these contemporary social and economic ambiguities. Under 'Visitor Opportunities' the stated goal in 1995 was to 'ensure that the range of visitor opportunities offered' reflected the Park's 'heritage character' and respected 'national park priorities to maintain ecological and cultural resource integrity' while at the same time complemented 'the opportunities with the region.' As a result of acrimonious debates over the townsite in the previous quarter century, a modest retreat appeared in 1995 by way of a compromise statement about the appropriate road to the future: 'Although Prince Albert National Park was originally established for reasons other than its wilderness values, these values have served to pro-

* George Whitter Jr. and Frank Poole, 'Recollections of Old Fishing Friends' in Dorell Taylor, ed., *Waskesiu Memories*, Vol. II. (Victoria: Classic Memoirs, 1999), 192

tect most of the Park in a wilderness state.' As proof that tourism was a tradition not to be ignored, appropriate new developments have taken place since 1988 such as the building of the destination Hawood Inn and the Sturgeon River Ranch near Big River on the 'wild west' side of the Park, well-suited to giving visitors a good look at the free ranging herd of bison. Also on the west side is the Province of Saskatchewan's beautiful Nesslin Lake Campground, a short distance outside of the Park. It provides the setting for the annual and popular Ness Creek Music Festival.

Since the mid-1990s, it has been the enterprise of Dorell Taylor to document the collective memory of many park users and residents.* In addition to preserving much warm and humorous local lore, these memoirs also demonstrate the wide range of opinion expressed about various policies over the years. Taken together they suggest that the early emphasis on recreation did not lead, in most minds, to any hostility towards the developing environmental concerns of the 1960s. On the contrary, local information was often seen to be instrumental to good policy decisions. One outcome of the previous squabbles was a new respect for local knowledge and in 2002 the Waskesiu Lake Community Council was put in place. Among other initiatives, the Council takes a close interest in the community plan that was approved in 2000.

National uncertainty over the deficit was far from over after 1995 and the search for financial solutions continued. The national parks were too sacred to ignore or offload to other governments, although some efforts were made to do so with some national historic sites. There was something else that might be done however, and that was to make the park system more financially autonomous as a quasi-crown corporation or agency. With passage of the Parks Canada Agency Act in 1998, a new life began for the Parks Branch. This was the latest in a series of shuffles since the late 1930s, but never before had the organization been quite so removed from public scrutiny or so tightly controlled. It was given a number of enhanced mandates, all detailed in various pieces of legislation. One element stressed the need for the national parks to pay more attention to neighbours on their borders.

When looking at details of that fine map of Peter Pond's, completed in 1785, one may note similarities with today's map. If, in Pond's day, local fur pelts were in low supply as a result of fur trade competition, the fur bearing animals have returned periodically. Native communities still surround the park. The bison which ranged in the vicinity of Pond's fort have returned after a lengthy absence. The forests and grasslands are reverting to a more normal relationship after the severe assaults by timber interests and fire. This

* See Dorell Taylor in the Bibliography.

Paignton Beach. A typical busy day of fun at the beach. Visitation in Prince Albert National Park has reached a quarter million each summer in the 21st century.

One of the unique features of the Park is the narrow-gauge railway used to portage boats past the rapids on the Kingsmere River between Waskesiu Lake and Kingsmere Lake. Human horsepower is the backbone of this memorable daylong venture for those heading to Grey Owl's cabin.

The Hanging Heart Lakes system on the way to Crean Lake.

is evidenced by the efforts of the Prince Albert Model Forest Association to promote a 'model forest' in the Park region. Initiatives to improve the quality of the fisheries inside and outside the Park have been underway for many years. New cooperative arrangements are developing with the various First Nation organizations, as at the Paspiwin Cultural Heritage Site. Boundary issues associated with wildlife movements in and out of the Park are being addressed by the Government of Saskatchewan and by volunteer organizations such as the Sturgeon River Plains Bison Stewards, Inc, which is concerned with the state of the herd released north of the Park in 1969 that subsequently drifted to the southwest. It is now a free-ranging herd numbering between 300 and 400 head and it migrates over a mix of private and public lands. This is a development of historic significance for it is one of the few free-ranging herds of bison in Canada. Wider interest in such wildlife restorations is indicated by the 2006 release of a herd on the Old Man on his Back Conservancy, south of Swift Current.

In many ways, even though Prince Albert National Park does not enjoy formal designation as a biosphere reserve, as do Waterton and Riding Mountain National Parks, there are indications that the Park is backing into just such a series of experimental and cooperative land use relationships by other means. The biosphere reserve concept is based on a highly-protected central core of land, such as a park or wilderness area, surrounded by graduated outer rings of more intense economic land use designations. Around Prince Albert National Park, what Irene Spry once described as 'the tragedy of the loss of the commons' is now being reversed, to some extent, by the reconfiguring of the Park as a special place among other connected special places and working landscapes. Within a formal biosphere reserve the assumption is that resident people, as in the past, must continue to make a productive living. The long term fostering of cooperative arrangements and policies are enthusiastically stressed in the 2007 Park Management Plan.

Park naturalist, musician, audio-visual wizard and former Chicago ad man, Joe Benge took a page from Grey Owl's book and put the urban world behind him in order to work for the National Parks of Canada. Here he holds a beaver kit in 1981.

These cooperative objectives are welcomed by the traditional visitors, business operators and the Park employees themselves, all of whom consider the reality of this place such an important part of their lives. It is from this general body that important support and arm's-length organizations have developed since the 1950s. Superintendents may come and go, too frequently in the minds of many, but a critical mass of goodwill always remains. The Friends of Prince Albert National Park organization, with its mandate to support Park initiatives and to help promote general heritage knowledge through its bookstore, celebrated its 25th anniversary in 2008. This body, for example, raised funds and completed the Grey Owl Beaver Lodge in 2005. Sharing the historic facility housing the Friends organization is the Waskesiu Heritage Museum, which has worked to collect and display important historic artifacts and displays of days gone by. An interesting achievement of the Museum is its conservation and display of one of the original Waskesiu shack tents. A committee of the Friends of Prince Albert National Park has guided development of an alternative to visiting the original 'Beaver Lodge' site by means of a scaled-down replica of the cabin now in their bookstore in Waskesiu. There, artifacts and memorabilia relevant to the life of Grey Owl may be

Grey Owl mending snowshoe in his cabin.

viewed in the 'Beaver Lodge' opened in 2005 and the Grey Owl and Anahareo Gallery which opened in 2006 thanks to funding by the Waskesiu Foundation and the Government of Saskatchewan.

One of the most interesting initiatives in recent years is the establishment of the Waskesiu Foundation, a unique institution among summer national park communities in Canada. As a registered charitable foundation its mission is to support recreational, social, cultural, and environmental facilities and activities that enhance the Waskesiu experience. The Foundation already has an impressive record of achievement thanks to the generosity of individual donors, including the refurbishing of the tennis courts, modernization of the Community Hall kitchen, sponsorship of the park bench programme and work in progress with Parks Canada as a partner on the restoration of the old bandstand lookout site and the updating of the historic Assembly Hall (Terrace Gardens). The early years of the 21st century at Prince Albert National Park reveal a re-energized local community at Waskesiu, anxious to draw upon, rather than eliminate, its traditions.

The Friends of Prince Albert National Park bookstore display of 'Beaver Lodge.' This shows the replica created in 2005, of the interior of Grey Owl's cabin at Ajawaan Lake.

The Waters Within

At the outset, we noticed the veteran fur trader Harold Kemp, explorer-like, entering what for him were the personally unknown waters within today's Prince Albert National Park. At its 80th anniversary, the Park still lies somewhat in the shadow of other better known Canadian parks, unknown to many even in its home province. Among those who know its charms, the Park inspires loyalty and a sense of community – it has remained 'Saskatchewan's Playground' in many respects. In keeping with changing attitudes, park use adjustments of many kinds have been made. The new Narrows campground, for example, is a modern Parks Canada ecological dream, designated as one of the first facilities totally run on solar power from street lamps to showers, a far cry from the location's historical significance as a fur trading post.

Today the Park remains a land of marshes, streams and lakes. Various kinds of tinkering have gone on with these waters since 1928, as was the case long before, either at the hand of humans or at the larger and more unpredictable hands of Mother Nature. As fears about global warming start to colour the public imagination, it is useful to think back to the main impulses behind the tradition of park establishments in Canada and its provinces. The larger parks were primarily put in place with a view to protecting headwaters, such as Algonquin Park in Ontario in 1893, the impressive system of provincial parks in British Columbia, Riding Mountain and Duck Mountain in Manitoba, Kejimkujik in Nova Scotia, and with the so-called 'national parks' established by the province of Quebec. It was essentially true of the early mountain national parks straddling the border region between Alberta and British Columbia, although there were some additional circumstances associated with railway and tourism enterprise. Most parks grew out of earlier designations associated with a new public land classification known as forest reserves where the need to preserve core watersheds in regions of ongoing timber exploitation suddenly registered on the minds of early land administrators such as Alexander Kirkwood. Thus, forest cover in the Beaver Hills west of Edmonton or the Waskesiu Hills north of Prince Albert, subtle as they are as heights of land, were seen to be serving an important purpose in stabilizing headwaters and being worthy of protection. Kemp noticed with some dismay just how much waterlogged muskeg was contained within what was being passed off to the public as a new national park. Kemp saw the local landscape more as a great sponge. If glaciers in the mountain parks to the west continue to shrink, the extensive network of prairie parks and reserves will be all the more important in the future as areas of water conservation and pristine environments for the education and enjoyment of future generations.

THE LAKE

Oh to be at Waskesiu
Now that summer's come

Just to see
Blue coloured sky
Above the lake and trees
Or to watch pelicans
Drift and shift their wings
Against a gentle breeze

Perhaps the friendship and faces
That appear each year
Draw us here
Personalities etched
With years of fun laughter
And trust

There is no better soul
Than those who shared
Your paddle and canoe
Your beach sand
Or Paignton fire

Stories of previous years
Summer days gone by
Time rolls effortlessly
One moon to another
The sun slips
Behind the clouds and hills
Each night
A stunning blaze of red glory

The story
Begins again at dawn
Loon's echo
Calling from the lake's heart

Come again
Come more often
Stay longer
But come
Share life's secrets
With friends
In nature's arms

Penned by R. Scott McCreath, 1995

Friends of Prince Albert National Park is a volunteer, charitable, non-profit organization made up of individuals, organizations and businesses dedicated to the stewardship of the natural and cultural resources of Prince Albert National Park. The 'Friends' promote public understanding, appreciation and enjoyment of the National Park.

Our mission is to support recreational, social, cultural, and environmental facilities and activities that enhance the Waskesiu experience.

Visit www.waskesiu.org

Friends of Prince Albert National Park Bookstore and home of the Waskesiu Heritage Museum.

Sources

The essential sources for the chapters are contained in the following references. For complete citations, see the listing in the Bibliography.

Chapter 1.

On glacial geology, see Lang, *Guide to the Geology of Prince Albert National Park* (1974); F.H. Edmunds, *Recession* (1962); and MacDonald (1971). On park prehistory see Forsman, *Prince Albert National Park Archaeological Survey* (1971); Gryba, *Final Report of the 1973 Archaeological Survey of Prince Albert National Park* (1974); and Meyer, 'The Prehistory of Northern Saskatchewan' in Epp and Dyck, eds., *Tracking Ancient Hunters* (1983), 141-70. On the 'Altithermal' concept see Meltzer, 'Human Responses' (1999), and Buchner, *Cultural Responses* (1980). On the general development of the fur trade in the west, see Morton, *A History of the Canadian West* (1973), Chapters 5-8. On Pond, see 'The Narrartive of Peter Pond' in Gates, ed., *Five Fur Traders* (1965) 11-59; Innis, *Peter Pond* (1930); and Wagner, Peter Pond (1955). On old Fort Sturgeon, see Thomson, 'The Return of Peter Pond' (2002), 17-127. On The Beaver Club, see Reed, *Masters* (1914), Ch.2. On the itinerary of David Thompson in the Green Lake area in 1798, see Tyrrell, ed., *Thompson's Narrative* (1916), lxxvii-lxxviii and Jenish, *Epic Wanderer* (2004), 108-10,

Chapter 2.

On the background of Palliser, see Spry, *The Palliser Expedition* (1963); on the role of the 1857 Commission of Enquiry into the Hudson's Bay Company, see Rich, *The Fur Trade* (1967), Ch. 15; for a distillation of the extensive literature on the decline of the bison, see Ogilvie, *The Park Buffalo* (1979). On the transition of the western territories into the Canadian Confederation, see Morton, *The Critical Years* (1964). The saga of Canadian Pacific Railway construction across Canada has been told thoroughly and entertainingly by Pierre Berton in several works. See Berton, *Great Railway* (1972). For background to the migration of some of the Montreal Lake Band, see McCarthy, *Grand Rapids* (1988), and Waiser, *Saskatchewan's Playground* (1989), 5-9. On the history of Treaty Six and Montreal Lake, see Ray, et al. *Bounty and Benevolence* (2000), 143-6. On the origins of the community of Prince Albert, see Abrams (1966), Ch. 1, and Zaslow, *Opening of the Canadian North* (1971), 71; on the post-1870 fur trade in Saskatchewan, see Ray, *Canadian Fur Trade* (1990), Chapters 2 and 3, and Zaslow (1971), 239-40. On the rise of the fishery see Waiser (1989), 11-12, and Rawson and Atton, *Biological Investigations* (1953), 7.

Chapter 3.

For the context of early expansion of natural resource resource development in the west and north of Prince Albert, see Berton, *The Promised Land* (1984), and Abrams, *Prince Albert* (1966), Ch. 11; Zaslow, *Northward Expansion* (1988), Ch. 1; Waiser, *Saskatchwan's Playground* (1989), Ch.2; and Waiser, *New Northwest* (1992). On the development of forest reserves see Knechtel, *Dominion* (1908) and on the Commission For Conservation, see Armstrong, 'Thomas Adams' in Gertler, ed., (1968) 17-35. On Harkin's career, see Taylor, 'J.B. Harkin' *Research Links* (1997), 5, and Harkin, 'Reflections' (1988). On employment in the early lumber camps see Kennedy, 'Reminiscences' (1966), and Shortt, *A Survey* (1977), 14-17. On the genesis of the Park concept, see Waiser (1989), Ch. 3.

Chapter 4.

On travel conditions in Northern Saskatchewan in the mid-1920s see *Vacations in Canada* (1927), 49-50. On the twentieth century fur trade in Northern Saskatchewan, see Zaslow, *Northward Expansion* (1988), 132; Keighley, *Trader, Tripper, Trapper* (1989); Brooks, *Strange Hunters* (1982); Kemp, *Northern Trader* (1956), Ch. 17. On the Treaty Lands agreement see Waiser, *Saskatchewan: A New History* (2006), 463-5. On the customs scandal of 1925 and the 1920s career of Mackenzie King, see Thompson and Seager, *Canada*, 1922-1939 (1985), 125, and Neatby, *William Lyon Mackenzie King* (1963). For Diefenbaker on the constitutional crisis of 1926, see Thompson and Seager (1985), 125. On the early planning of the townsite, see Lothian, *A History*, Vol. 1(1976), 67, and Waiser, *Saskatchewan's Playground* (1989), 37-8; on place name changes, see Waiser (1989), 41 and Barry, *People Places* (2003). On boundary changes see Shortt , *A Survey* (1977), 110-14, and Waiser (1989), 63, 104.

Chapter 5.

On numbers of relief workers at the park, see Waiser, *Saskatchewan's Playground* (1989) 62, and *Park Prisoners* (1995), 92-4. On the golf course, see Lothian, *A History*, Vol. 3. (1979), 99-100, and Burton, 'Who designed?' (2007). On the arrival of bison at Prince Albert, see Ogilvie, *Park Buffalo* (1979), 32 and Waiser (1989), 94. On improvements in the park in the 1930s, see Waiser (1989), Ch. 6. On artistic developments at Emma Lake, see Snyder, 'Art in Northern Saskatchewan' (1980) and Dillow, Saskatchewan (1971). On Grey Owl see the entries under Grey Owl, Anahareo, Dickson, Mitcham, Rashley and Smith. On Anahareo, see her *My Life* (1940), Ch. 1 and Ch. 12; and *Devil in Deerskins* (1972), 107-34, 156-76. On Anahareo in old age see Schuyler, 'Still Bucking' (1980) and see 'Grey Owl's Widow'(1983). On Rilke's original comments on 'the two solitudes' see Rilke, *Letters* (1986),78. On the 'Smokejumpers' see *Saskatchewan's Forests* (1955), 52-54. On pelicans and cormorants, see Soper, *The Birds of Prince Albert* (1952), 2, 16-18.

Chapter 6.

On church services at Waskesiu, see *Summer Program* (1958), 57. On Diefenbaker's changing views and the shack tent issue see Waiser, *Saskatchewan's Playground* (1989), 42, 125-31. On various conflicts within late twentieth century national parks administration, see Searle, *Phantom Parks*, (2001), Ch. 5. On the conflict between parks and tourism, see Downie and Pert, eds., *Parks and Tourism* (1982). On population, see Fuller, *Earth Inc.* (1973). On wildlife in the park see Soper, *The Mammals of Prince Albert* (1952) and Henry, *Red Fox* (1986).

Chapter 7.

On developing parks policy in the 1990s, and the concept of 'ecological integrity' see Parks Canada, *Into the Future* (1996), and Grumbine, 'Reflections' (1997). On various conflicts within late twentieth century national parks administration, see Searle, *Phantom Parks*, (2001), Ch. 5. On the effects of programme review, see Toner, 'Environment Canada's Continuing Roller Coaster Ride' in Swimmer, ed. (1996). On park fees see Canadian Heritage. *News Release*, '1995'. For Harkin's general views see Harkin, 'Reflections' *Park News*, (1988), 11 and Taylor, 'Defining National Parks' (1997), 5. On policy issues, see Searle, *Phantom Parks*, (2001), Ch. 5. On wildlife cycles and history, see MacDonald, 'Is Wildlife History, Bunk?' (1999). On the spruce budworm issue see Woodly, *Spruce Budworm* (2002). On timber history in Prince Albert National Park see Shortt, *A Survey* (1977), 13-19, 114-30. On Mintzburg, see Bernhut, 'In Conversation' (2000). On Rohe, see Rohe, *A Bicentennial Malthusian Essay* (1997). On the establishment of a Waskesiu Community Plan and the Waskesiu Advisory Council see Parks Canada, *Management Plan*, (1995), 39, and Parks

Canada, *Waskesiu Community Plan* (2000). On the Sturgeon River Plains Bison Stewards Inc., see panp.info.@pc.g.c.ca. On the model forest, see Goode, Report. (1995). On the biosphere reserve at Waterton, see MacDonald, *Where the Mountains*, (2000), 155-58, and on the general objectives of the Biosphere Reserve movement, see Eidsvik, 'Canada' in Dearden and Rollins, (1993), 279-81. On the fate of the 'commons', see Spry, 'Tragedy' in Getty and Lussier, eds., (1983), 203-28. On the importance of forest reserves in the early Canadian park movement, see Lambert and Pross (1967), 165-73.

Bibliography

Abrams, Gary. *Prince Albert: The First Century, 1866-1966*. Saskatoon: Modern Press, 1966.

Anahareo [Gertrude Bernard]. *My Life with Grey Owl*. London: Peter Davies, 1940.

________. *Devil in Deerskins*: *My Life with Grey Owl*. Toronto: New Press, 1972.

Armstrong, Alan H. 'Thomas Adams and the Commission of Conservation' in Gertler, ed. (1968), 17-35

Barka, N and A. *Archaeology and the Fur Trade: The Excavation of Sturgeon Fort, Saskatchewan*. History and Archaeology, 7. Ottawa: National Historic Parks and Sites Branch, 1976.

Barry, Bill. *People Places: Contemporary Saskatchewan Place Names*. Regina: People Places Publishing Ltd. 1997.

Belaney, Archibald. See Grey Owl.

Bernhut, Stephen, 'In Conversation: Henry Mintzberg' *Ivey Business Journal* (Oct. 2000), 18-23

Berton, Pierre. *The Great Railway: Illustrated*. Toronto: McClelland and Stewart, 1972.

___________. *The Promised Land: Settling the West*, 1896-1914. Toronto: McClelland and Stewart, 1984.

Brooks, John A. *Strange Hunters: Life and Adventures in Northern Saskatchewan During the 1920's and 30's*. Port Alberni: Coast Printers, 1982.

Buchner, Anthony P. *Cultural Responses to Altithermal (Atlantic) Climate along the Eastern Margins of the North American Grasslands, 5500 to 3000 B.C.* Ottawa: Archaeological Survey of Canada, Paper No. 97. 1980.

Burton, Randy, 'Who designed Waskesiu Golf Course?' *Saskatoon Star Phoenix*, Sept. 4, 2007.

Canadian Heritage. News Release. '1995 fees for national parks and national historic sites' Ottawa. April, 4, 1995.

Dearden, Philip and Rollins, Rick, eds. *Parks and Protected Areas in Canada: Planning and Management*. Toronto: Oxford University Press, 1993.

Dickson, Lovat. *The Green Leaf: A Memorial to Grey Owl*. London: Lovat Dickson Ltd. 1939.

____________. *Wilderness Man: The Strange Story of Grey Owl*. Toronto: Macmillan, 1973.

Dillow, Nancy. 'Introduction' *Saskatchewan: Art and Artists*. Regina: Norman MacKenzie Art Gallery/ Regina Public Library Art Gallery, 1971.

Downie, Bruce and Peart, Bob. *Parks and Tourism: Progress or Prostitution?* Victoria: National and Pro vincial Parks Association of Canada. 1982.

Edmunds, F.H. *Recession of Wisconsinan Glacier from Central Saskatchewan*. Petroleum and Natural Gas Branch. Geology Division, Report No. 67. Regina: Department of Mineral Resources, 1962.

Eidsvik, Hal. 'Canada, Conservation and Protected Areas' in Dearden and Rollins, eds. (1993), 273-90

Epp, Henry T. and Ian Dyck, eds. *Tracking Ancient Hunters*. Regina: Saskatchewan Archaeological Society, 1983.

Frith, Shanna D. *Trail Guide: Prince Albert National Park*. Waskesiu: Friends of Prince Albert National Park. 1997.

Fuller, R. Buckminster. *Earth, Inc* (1947). Garden City: Doubleday, 1973.
Gates, Charles, M., ed. 'The Narrative of Peter Pond' in: *Five Fur Traders of the Northwest*. Minneapolis: Minnesota Historical Society Press, 1965, 11-59
Gertler, L.O., ed. *Planning the Canadian Environment*. Montreal: Harvest House 1968.
Getty, Ian and Lussier, Antoine, eds. *As Long as the Sun Shines and the Water Flows*. Vancouver: University of British Columbia Press, 1983.
Grey Owl. [Archibald Belaney]. *The Adventures of Sajo and her Beaver People*. London: Lovat Dickson and Thompson Ltd. 1935.
________. *Men of the Last Frontier*. London: Country Life Ltd. 1931.
________. *Pilgrims of the Wild*. Foreword by Hugh Eayrs. London: Lovat Dickson Ltd. 1935.
________. *Tales of an Empty Cabin*. London: Lovat Dickson Ltd. 1936.
'Grey Owl's Widow' *B.C. Citizen*, July 25, 1983.
Grumbine, Edward. 'Reflections on "What is Ecosystem Management" ' *Conservation Biology* 11(1) (1997), 41-47
Harkin, J.B. *The Origin and Meaning of the National Parks of Canada*. Ottawa: National Parks Branch. 1957.
__________. 'Our Need for National Parks' *Canadian Alpine Journal*, 9: (1918), 98-106
__________. 'Reflections of a Park Administrator' *Park News*, 23(5) (1988), 11
Henry, David R. *The Red Fox*. Washington, DC: Smithsonian Institution Press, 1986.
Innis, Harold. *Peter Pond: Fur Trader and Adventurer*. Toronto: Irwin and Gordon, 1930.
Jenish, D'Arcy. *Epic Wanderer: David Thompson and the Mapping of the Canadian West*. Toronto. Double day, 2003.
Kemp, H.S.M. *Northern Trader*. Toronto: Ryerson Press, 1956.
Keighley, Sydney A. *Trader, Tripper, Trapper: The Life of a Bay Man*. With Renee Fossett Jones and David K. Riddle. (Winnipeg: Rupert's Land Research Centre / Watson and Dwyer, 1989.
Kennedy, Allan. 'Reminiscences of a Lumberjack' *Saskatchewan History*, 19 (1) (1966), 24-34
Knechtel, A. *The Dominion Forest Reserves*. Forestry Branch. Bull. No. 3 Ottawa: Department of the Interior. 1908.
Lambert, Richard S. and Pross, Paul. *Renewing Nature's Wealth*. Toronto: Ontario Department of Lands and Forests, 1967.
Lang, A.H. *Guide to the Geology of Prince Albert National Park*. Geological Survey of Canada. Misc. Report, 21. Ottawa: Department of Energy, Mines and Resources, 1974.
Lothian, W. F. *A History of Canada's National Parks*. Ottawa: Parks Canada. 1976-1982. 4 Vol.
McCarthy, Martha. *Grand Rapids, Manitoba*. Papers in Manitoba History, No. 1. Winnipeg: Manitoba Culture, Heritage and Recreation: Historic Resources Branch, 1988.
MacDonald, Graham A. 'Is Wildlife History Bunk? Reflections on I.J.M. Robertson' Paper presented to the Symposium, *Learning from the Past: A Historical Look at Mountain Ecosystems*. Revelstoke: Columbia Mountains Institute of Applied Ecology. 1999.
___________________. *Where the Mountains Meet the Prairies: A History of Waterton Country*. Calgary: University of Calgary Press, 2001.
MacDonald, Robert. *Canada I: Years and Years Ago: The Romance of Canadian History*. Vancouver: Evergreen Press, 1971.
Meltzer, David J. 'Human Responses to Middle Holocene (Altithermal) Climates on the North American Great Plains' *Quaternary Research*, 52 (1999), 404-16
Mitcham, Allison. 'Grey Owl in the Park' *Northward Journal*, 17 (1980), 7-11

Morton, Arthur S. *A History of the Canadian West to 1870-71*. 2nd. ed. Lewis G. Thomas, ed. Toronto: University of Toronto Press, 1973.
Morton, W.L. *The Critical Years: The Union of British North America*, 1957-1873. Toronto: McClelland and Stewart, 1964.
Neatby, H. Blair. *William Lyon Mackenzie King, 1924-1932*. Toronto: University of Toronto Press, 1963.
Ogilvie, Sheilagh C. *The Park Buffalo*. Toronto: National and Provincial Parks Association, 1979.
______________. *W.J.Oliver: Life Through a Master's Lens*. Calgary: Glenbow Museum, 1984.
Parks Canada Into the Future. Ottawa: Department of Canadian Heritage, 1996.
Rashley, R.E. 'Grey Owl and the Authentic Frontier' *English Quarterly*, 4 (3) (1971), 57-64
Rawson, D.S. and Atton, F.M. *Biological Investigations and Fisheries Management at Lac La Ronge, Saskatchwan*. Regina: Saskatchewan Department of Natural Resources, 1953.
Ray, Arthur J. *The Canadian Fur Trade in the Industrial Age*. Toronto: University of Toronto Press, 1990.
Ray, Arthur J., Miller, Jim, and Tough, Frank. *Bounty and Benevolence: A History of Saskatchewan Treaties*. Montreal: McGill-Queen's University Press, 2000.
Reed, C.B. *Masters of the Wilderness*. Chicago: University of Chicago Press, 1914.
Rich, E.E. *The Fur Trade and the Northwest to 1857*. Toronto: McClelland and Stewart, 1967.
Rilke, Rainer Maria. *Letters to a Young Poet*. Stephen Mitchell, Trans. New York: Random House, 1986.
Rohe, John F. *A Bicentennial Malthusian Essay: Conservation, Population and the Indifference to Limits*. Traverse City: Rhodes and Easton, 1997.
Saskatchewan's Forests. Regina: Department of Natural Resources, 1955.
Schuyler, Lynne, 'Still Bucking the Wind' *Today* (May 24, 1980), 8-9
Searle, Rick. *Phantom Parks: The Struggle to Save Canada's National Parks*. Toronto: Key Porter Books, 2000.
Shortt, James. *A Survey of the Human History of Prince Albert National Park*, 1887-1945. Manuscript Report 239. Ottawa: Parks Canada. Department of Indian and Northern Affairs. 1977.
Smith, Donald B. *From the Land of Shadows: The Making of Grey Owl*. Saskatoon: Western Prairie Producer Books, 1990.
Snyder, Gordon, 'Art in Northern Saskatchewan' *Northward Journal*, 17 (1980), 19-28
Soper, J. Dewey. *The Birds of Prince Albert National Park*. Wildlife Management Bulletin. Series 2. No. 4. Ottawa: Canadian Wildlife Service. 1952.
____________. *The Mammals of Prince Albert National Park*. Wildlife Management Bulletin. Series 1. No. 5. Ottawa: Canadian Wildlife Service. 1952.
Spry, Irene, *The Palliser Expedition*. Toronto: Macmillan, 1963.
Spry, Irene. 'The Tragedy of the Loss of the Commons' in Getty and Lussier, eds. (1983), 203-28
Summer Program, 1958. Waskesiu. Prince Albert National Park. Waskesiu Board of Trade: 1958.
Swimmer, G., ed. *How Ottawa Spends, 1996-97: Life Under the Knife*. Ottawa: Carlton University Press, 1997.
Taylor, C.J. 'Defining National Parks: J.B. Harkin and the National Parks Branch' *Research Links*, 5(1) (1997), 5
Taylor, Dorell, ed. *Waskesiu Memories*. Victoria: Classic Memoirs, 1998-2003. 3 Vol.
Thompson, John H. and Allen Seager. *Canada, 1922-1939: Decades of Discord*. Toronto: McClelland and Stewart, 1985.
Thomson, Sharon. 'The Return of Peter Pond: Summary and Analysis of Cultural Resources From Sturgeon Fort, Saskatchewan' *The Manitoba Archaeological Journal*, 12:1 (2002), 17-127
Toner, Glen. 'Environment Canada's Continuing Roller Coaster Ride' in Swimmer, ed., (1997).

Tyrrell, J.B. ed. *David Thompson's Narrative of his Explorations in Western North America, 1784-1812*. Toronto: Champlain Society, 1916.

Vacations in Canada: A Handbook of Information for Tourists and Sportsmen. Ottawa: Department of the Interior. 1927.

Wagner, Henry R. *Peter Pond: Fur Trader and Explorer* (New Haven: Yale University Press, 1955).

Waiser, Bill. *Park Prisoners: The Untold Story of Western Canada's National Parks, 1915-1946*. Saskatoon: Fifth House, 1995.

_________. *Saskatchwan: A New History*. Calgary: Fifth House, 2006.

_________. *Saskatchewan's Playground*. Saskatoon: Fifth House, 1989.

_________. *The New Northwest: The Photographs of the Frank Crean Expeditions, 1908-1909*. Saskatoon: Fifth House, 1993.

Waskesiu Community Plan. Ottawa: Parks Canada. 2000.

Wettlaufer, Boyd. *The Mortlach Site*. Regina: Department of Natural Resources, 1955.

Wiens, Alfred, ed. *La Ronge: Our Roots*. La Ronge: Lakeland Press, 1981.

Woodly, Stephen. *Spruce Budworm in Prince Albert National Park-Policy Analysis* (Ottawa: Parks Canada, 2002).

Zaslow, Morris. *The Northward Expansion of Canada, 1914-1967*. Toronto: McClelland and Stewart, 1988,

132

Acknowledgments and Illustration Credits

The authors thank the following for their assistance.

Kiley Bear, Prince Albert City Hall; Jim Beckel, Friesens Printers; Blair Barbeau, Kenderdine Gallery, University of Saskatchewan; Michael Benoit and Marlon Janzen, Royal Saskatchewan Museum; Suzanne Bergevin, Katharine Kinnear, Parks Canada Agency; Ken Dahl, Saskatchewan Archives Board; Jacinthe Duval, La Société Historique de Saint-Boniface; Dave Edwards, Edwards, Edwards, McEwen, Architects; Al Harvey, The Slide Farm Inc.; Dan Krasemann, DRK Photo; Ione Langois, Waskesiu Heritage Museum; James LaBounty, Photographer; Adria Lund, Glenbow Archives; Murdine McCreath; Bill McDonald, Peter Pond Society; Adrian Glasgow and Bill McKay, Prince Albert Masonic Lodge; Carla Flaman, Carlene Gorecki, Murray Peterson, Prince Albert National Park; Robert Paul, Diefenbaker Canada Centre; Sharon Thomson, Western Service Centre Archaeological Unit, Parks Canada Agency; Dorell Taylor; Jim Webb.

For assistance in reviewing the manuscript, many thanks to Susie Sparks, who helped us get the words right, and Janice MacKinnon, Aritha van Herk, Scott and James McCreath. Finally, a heartfelt thanks to designer Lori Nunn, who cheerfully provided constant assistance and wise guidance, well beyond the call of duty.

Photo and Art Credits listed by source, title and page of appearance.

Archives and Libraries Canada. Cree peoples by Robert Hood (C-038951), 11; Beach at Waskesiu (PA-049875), rear cover; Louis LaVallée and Grandson (PA-049784), 22 ; W.L.M. King at Opening Ceremony (C-051825), 34; King's cabin (PA-178404)

Authors' collections. 1, 18, 39, 40, 41, 42, 43, 45, 58, 59, 60, 64, 69, 70, 72, 76, 77, 79, 80, 82, 84, 85, 88, 93

Banff National Park. Webster Collection: Workers, 37

Bantle, Jason Leo: Road Warriors, 73
Barka, N. and A.: Sturgeon Fort Archaeology, 10
Beaver Magazine: RCMP cariole, 44
Canada. Department of the Interior: J.B. Harkin, 20
Canada Pictures Ltd: John Diefenbaker (JGD 398), 69
Canadian National Railways: Women by lake, 57
Christie, Mary and Liam: Stanley Mission, 12, Waskesiu Lake sunset, 92
Douglas, Carole: Terrace Gardens and Waskesiu Terriers, 46
DRK Photo. Sedona AZ: 'Red Fox' © Stephen J. Krasemann/DRK Photo, 73
Edwards, Edwards, McEwen, Architects, Saskatoon: Waskesiu Clubhouse, 40 (bottom)
Geological Survey of Canada: Golf Course, 6
Glenbow Museum and Archives: W.L. Oliver Coll. Grey Owl (NA-4868-208), 49; Anahareo, Grey Owl, William Oliver (NA-4868-202), 50; Grey Owl paddling canoe, Lake Ajawaan (NA-4868-210), 52; Grey Owl mending snowshoe (NA-3164-351), 87
Harvey, Al. The Slide Farm Inc.: Narrows, 7; bison, 27; Grey Owl's cabin, 47; moose feeding, 81; Joe Benge, 86
Kenderdine, Augustus (Private Collection): Waskesiu Lake, front cover.
Lovat Dickson Ltd.: Grey Owl, 51
Manitoba Archives. Keighly Collection: Alan Nunn, 30
Muir, Brad: McCreaths near Sturgeon River, Prince Albert National Park, 103
Nunn, Lori & Graeme: Entrance sign, iii; Park Twin Theatre, 67
Oliver, W.L. (Private Collection): Mary LaVallée, 22
Parks Canada Agency, Photo 8 Parks Canada/W. Oliver: Men poling, vii; Superintendent James Wood and family, 38
Perkins, Wayne: Canoeist, 89
Peter Davies Ltd: Anahareo with bear, 53; Anahareo and Dawn, 54; Cover of *My Life with Grey Owl*, 55
Peter Pond Society, Milford CT: Pond's Beaver Club Medal, 11
Pinder, Kathy: Hanging Heart Lakes, 85
Prince Albert National Park of Canada: Besant Culture Projectile Point (PA111), 7; Portrait of T.C. Davis by Nicolas de Grandmaison, 26
Prince Albert Masonic Lodge: Prince Albert Masonic Temple, 25
Royal Saskatchewan Museum: Pelicans and cormorants. Fred Lahrman and R.D. Symons, 62
Saskatchewan Archives Board: Children at Green Lake, 19
Taylor, Dorell: Shack tent, 45; Women in camp kitchen, 59
Webb, James R.: Ancient Waskesiuians (Watercolour 2008), 8
Winnipeg Free Press, Arch Dale Collection: Bennett cartoon, 37

Map Credits

Archives and Libraries Canada: Peter Pond's Map. 1785 (Detail), 10
Canada, Department of Mines and Technical Surveys: Rupert's Land, 13
Canada, Department of the Interior: Prince Albert National Park. 1936, 30
Canada, Department of Natural Resources: Prince Albert National Park. 1952, 63
Canadian Parks and Wilderness Association, Saskatchewan Chapter: Orientation map, viii
Prince Albert Chamber of Commerce: Waskesiu Townsite. 1958, 66
Saskatchewan Archives Board. Sturgeon Lake Forest Reserve. 1924, 23

Index

About the Authors

Graham MacDonald has lived in many different parts of Canada. He has worked as a teacher, librarian, author, park planner and historian. Between 1982 and 1990 he was principal of *The Crocus Group, Heritage Planning Associates* in Winnipeg. He is retired from Parks Canada where he worked as a historian. Currently he lives and works as a consultant in Victoria, BC. This photo is Graham at the Burgess Shale World Heritage Site in Yoho National Park.

Grit McCreath has been an educator for over three decades in Saskatchewan, Ontario and Alberta. She has worked extensively in the not-for-profit sector and is currently on the Senate of the University of Saskatchewan and a Friends of Prince Albert National Park board member. Her husband, Scott, introduced her to the Park in the early 70's. They have two sons, Andy and James, and as a family they have always spent their summer vacations at Waskesiu. Grit and Scott are pictured near the Sturgeon River on the west side of Prince Albert National Park.